ESTATE PLANNING

ESTATE

PLANNING

A WORKBOOK FOR CHRISTIANS

Richard D. Bailey

ILLUSTRATIONS BY CAROLYN BROWN

ABINGDON PRESS   NASHVILLE

Estate Planning: A Workbook for Christians

Library of Congress Cataloging in Publication Data

Bailey, Richard D. (Richard Douglas), 1934-
  Estate planning, a workbook for Christians.
  1. Estate planning—United States. I. Title.
KF750.Z9B33   343.7305'3   347.30353   81-14907   AACR2

ISBN 0-687-12004-7 (pbk.)

MANUFACTURED BY THE PARTHENON PRESS AT
NASHVILLE, TENNESSEE, UNITED STATES OF AMERICA

Dedicated to my family—Ellen, my wife, and my children, Mark, Kimberly, and Kent Bailey—my associates, and friends, especially Tom Rieke, Hal Measley, Harry Underwood, and Susan Lang, who supported me in the preparation of this workbook and who believe in the stewardship of accumulating resources.

Dover, Delaware
January 1982

Contents

— ont of date now.

Foreword

by Thomas C. Rieke

The Bible places a high premium on good management practices by the people of God.

The scriptures of Old and New Testament alike abound with principles and examples of sound management. In countless settings, God brings something into being and then relinquishes control of it into the hands of the people he has formed. Intently, the student of the Sacred Word reads on to see how well the creature handles the entrustment of the Creator.

Genesis begins as God is about his work of making the world, shaping it to divine specifications. No sooner has it all been pronounced "good" than it is given over to the management of the people God has made. Revelation concludes with the judgment that those who have conquered (managed well) will reign eternally with the One who is King of kings and Lord of lords.

In between these pictures of human possibility are scores of illustrations of the same principles at work. The God of Israel effects the rescue of his captive people from Egypt and then entrusts them to the management of Moses. The inhabitants of the Promised Land are defeated, the kingdom established, and David comes to the throne to manage the affairs of the people of God. Amid trying circumstances, the prophets were entrusted with the Word of the Lord, and their management of its message was crucial.

The Gospel writers record numerous instances of Jesus' teaching in the form of parables. And the point of most of them relates to the matter of management. A garment is torn and needs to be patched—how best can it be done? Oil is in short supply for wedding attendants—how shall they handle the situation? Light is provided—what shall be done with it?

In a classic trilogy, three things are missing—a sheep, a coin, and a boy. What is the loser to do? A good manager will know that rescue and joy and acceptance will be the order of the day. Clearly, the Scriptures mean to tell us that God wants us to be good managers as well.

Perhaps nowhere is that fact more pointed than in the story of the person of considerable means who left three of his servants in charge of some of his resources. Two of them took their entrustment and managed it in such a way as to produce a yield of 100 percent. The third returned his intact. Nothing was missing, and no dishonesty was involved. Nothing had happened. There had been a breakdown in management. His portion was quickly recovered and given to the person who had produced a top return on the largest sum. Jesus puts into the mouth of the wealthy man words that clearly say that those who do well with what they have been given will be given more. That is a high premium on good management.

The people of God in this day have not eluded the necessity of being good managers of the things entrusted to them. Biblical mandates for management belong to every generation—including this one. We simply must do well with the things committed to our care in order to qualify as workers who have no need of being ashamed.

Richard Bailey has written a book that will help us all attain the level of achievement needed in a critical area of management. Volumes have been dedicated to helping us manage current resources. He has ventured into an almost uncharted area to help us manage our accumulating resources.

And he has produced a remarkable piece of work that puts all of us in his debt. He has avoided the extremes of simplicity, which may lead to inaccuracy, and complexity, which may lead to neglect. Richard tells us clearly what we must do and how we must do it when it comes to the management of our accumulations. Property, taxes, insurance, trusts, social security—and a host of equally complex subjects—march across the pages of this book for all to see, appreciate, and use to their benefit.

Procrastination and ignorance are not the tools of a good manager. This book banishes them from the experience of the Christian and replaces them with helpful guidance. No one now can plead an absence of knowledge. Persons who want to handle wisely the trusts given them have all the needed tools at their disposal here. These equip the good manager to know what can and should be done. An attorney can supply the legal competence necessary to turn wisdom into action.

If you knew Richard Bailey, you would not be the least bit surprised at his book. It is as direct, concise, and thoughtful as is he. When you talk with him, you sense immediately that he likes things to be done decently and in order. If you follow his career, you know that he is concerned that Christian people know how to manage their affairs in a Christlike manner.

As the people of God, we have long been preoccupied with the management of our current earnings. We are learning how to manage these while largely ignorant of the ways we can manage our accumulating earnings and pass them on to others. No longer! This book, in the hands of wise managers, will produce thoughtful, prudent plans that will acknowledge their makers as obedient followers of Christ.

One of the first copies of this book will be found in our home. I have read the manuscript, reviewed the contents, and know how much we need the help contained here. We, too, want to hear that word of approval—Well done, good and faithful steward. Enter into the joy of your Lord. Indeed!

Thomas C. Rieke
Assistant General Secretary
for Stewardship
General Board of Discipleship
The United Methodist Church

Foreword

by Harold F. Measley, Jr., Esquire

To cite that familiar quotation, two things are certain in life—death and taxes. However, it is amazing how many people fail to plan properly their estate.

As a tax attorney who is heavily involved in estate planning and administration, I wholeheartedly welcome this workbook by Richard D. Bailey. It contains an excellent explanation for the layperson of the many legal and tax considerations in planning an estate.

I have learned from my legal practice that the vast majority of clients have no understanding of what happens with their property after they die. The documents that we lawyers must prepare further add to the layperson's confusion because, unfortunately, laws (especially tax laws) are becoming more complicated. Richard Bailey's book will go a long, long way in dispelling much of this confusion.

As Richard Bailey states in this book, there are many people who do not have a will, let alone have done any serious estate planning. I shudder to think how many people who did not have a will, have prepared their own, used a form from a book, or had a will prepared by an attorney who was not well versed in estate planning. When a person's estate has not been properly planned, in the vast number of cases, the ones who will be adversely affected are that person's family; the ones who gain are the federal and state treasuries.

This is the first book I have seen that will give you a sound, basic understanding of estate planning. After you have finished the book, you will have everything you need to begin to plan your estate by seeking competent professional advice. Use this book and start today to arrange your affairs so that your family will receive, after your death, the maximum amount of your property with the least amount of worry and unnecessary problems.

HAROLD F. MEASLEY, JR., ESQUIRE
WILMINGTON, DELAWARE

Overview

Estate planning, including the making of a *will,* is the paramount legal concern of the American family. Less than half of the persons related to churches have written a will. Far less have done any serious planning of their estate.

Why?

The biggest reason is procrastination. People simply put it off.

There are other reasons. Associating the making of a will and planning one's estate with death is a primary reason. Fear that the cost will be too high or distrust of attorneys are other reasons. Then there are those who believe their estate is too small.

All these reasons may seem important, but, in reality, they are not. They are just not true. Planning one's estate is for the living. It is not something that should be left for the last few years of life. Making a will or taking steps in estate planning will not cause you to die any sooner. And it probably will not make you live longer; it can, however, give you peace of mind.

Cost? Estate-planning costs vary, depending on how complicated the estate is and how much of an attorney's time is used. Include the time to prepare a will or update an existing one. You can check cost by telephoning the local bar association or several attorneys in your community. You will not get an exact fee estimate until the attorney can determine your particular needs. However, you should be able to get a low/high cost range. Adequate planning and a properly prepared estate plan are essential. Without them, the expense will be far more costly to your estate and your heirs.

Distrust of attorneys is not a valid reason. Many attorneys can write wills, but few have become skilled in designing an estate plan. There are good estate-planning attorneys; you will need to take time and look before making a selection.

Planning your estate is important. It assures that what you want done will happen. It does not leave things to chance. It protects what you have worked hard to obtain. It allows you to implement your wishes and beliefs.

As you plan, you will discuss with your attorney:

* the size of your estate
* your property and how it is owned
* your family and other beneficiaries
* your life insurance program
* how taxes relate to the transfer of property
* any gifts you intend to make during your lifetime
* charitable gifts you wish to make
* your need for a properly written will
* records you will need to assemble
* keeping your estate plan current

From the Christian perspective, estate planning offers something more. It offers a fulfillment of Christian responsibility. A Christian understands that all life is a gift from God. What you do with this gift is important. Wise use of your accumulating resources is part of that trust from God. Christian estate planning will take into account adequate support of your family and continued support of the ministries of Christ after you are gone.

CAUTION: The purpose of this workbook is to help persons consider the various options and gather the information necessary in planning their estate. It is not intended to give legal advise or opinions. Persons desiring estate planning need professional help and should seek the services of a competent attorney.

I. Estate Planning

What Is Estate Planning?

Estate planning is an ordering of human affairs. It is designing a plan for managing, preserving, and disposing of property during life, at times of disability or emergency, and at death. And to accomplish this with the least tax obligation.

Most persons are not knowledgeable about the technical aspects of estate planning. But they do have definite ideas about what should happen to what they own. If you do not plan, what you intend probably will not happen. If you do not have a plan, your state has one for you. If you die *intestate* (that is, without a valid will), your property will be distributed according to the formula your state has developed.

Estate planning is the responsibility of every Christian. It is our concern to plan for the security of our families and to provide for the work of Christ in the world. The stewardship of accumulating resources—the wise management and use of our assets—is part of the fulfillment of our mission and ministry.

Our society has laws and taxes that affect whatever planning you do and may restrict your disposition of accumulating resources. These laws are numerous and often complex. An estate-planning team headed by a competent attorney can provide the assistance you need. You might choose an accountant, bank trust officer, financial advisor, life insurance underwriter, and development officer to join you and your attorney on the team.

Each of these persons has skills that are important in developing your estate plan. Your accountant knows your financial affairs. A bank trust officer can help if your plan involves trusts. Life insurance underwriters can tailor an insurance program to fit your goals. A financial advisor can survey any investments you have. A development officer from a church-related foundation or charity can assist in planning your charitable giving program. The key person you will need to select is an attorney.

Selecting an Attorney

There is no infallible way to choose an attorney, but remember that, although many attorneys can write wills, few are skilled in designing an estate plan. Each year there are thousands of income tax, *estate tax,* and *gift tax* rulings. Only those who are serious about estate planning will keep up with all these.

Where do you begin your search? Two publications *The Bar Register* and *The Martindale-Hubbell Law Directory* (available in many libraries and law offices) provide a good starting point. Of course, not everyone listed specializes in estate planning. But you increase your chances of finding a competent attorney. Virtually all the lawyers in the United States are listed in *The Martindale-Hubbell Law Directory,* and their legal ability is rated. The biographical section may contain information about those who have written or lectured on estate planning.

If you live near a law school, you might inquire about the names of those skilled in estate planning. A bank trust officer could also make suggestions, as could probate judges and clerks.

When doing your research, do not hesitate to ask an attorney about his or her experience in this area. A good attorney's library should contain a loose-leaf service on income taxes, gift taxes, and estate taxes. All federal tax decisions should also be available. These are clues to an attorney's competence in estate planning. Your goal is to find an estate-planning attorney who can do the job. The cost of drafting your estate plan can more than be made up in what a competent attorney will save in taxes.

Making a Will

A properly written will is the basic document in any estate plan. It is a legal declaration of what you want done with your estate, or property, at death. Of course, there is a lot more to estate planning than arranging for the transfer of property at death. And the fact that you have a will does not mean you have an estate plan. A will should reflect the planning you have done and assure that your plan will be carried out.

In a **will** you can:

* Name the *executor/executrix* and an *alternate executor/executrix* (if your first choice is unable to serve at that time) to manage and settle your estate according to your wishes. Expense can be saved by not requiring the executor to furnish a *bond.*
* Name a *guardian* for minor children. If your spouse survives you, the court will usually appoint the spouse as guardian, and the will can dispense with any bond the court might require. If you and your spouse should die in a common accident, your choice of a guardian becomes very important.
* Name a trusted individual, bank, or trust company to manage your investments.
* Create trusts to protect the interests of surviving spouse, children, and others.
* Make gifts to your church and other charitable causes.
* Plan for the payment of death taxes and, if you like, specify from whose share of the estate they are to be paid.
* Establish the order of death if you and your spouse die simultaneously in a common disaster, to assure the order for distribution of property.

As you plan your estate, your attorney will make sure both you and your spouse have a will that reflects and supports your plan. If you already have wills, the attorney will make sure they are updated or rewritten as necessary.

When your will is completed to your satisfaction, you will sign it in the presence of witnesses. Two witnesses are required by most states; a few require three.

You should keep your will in a safe place, where it will be easily found upon death. If you keep it in your safe-deposit box, be aware that some states seal the box upon death, and a court order is required to have it opened. Some attorneys keep wills for their clients. A bank trust department may do the same.

You should review your will and estate plan periodically. **Reviewing** should take place when changes occur or when you contemplate changes in:

* jobs
* the family—births, marriages, divorces, deaths
* residence—especially a move to another state
* the law—federal or state
* income—an unexpected windfall or substantial salary increase
* the estate plan
* charitable giving intentions

A *codicil,* the legal word for "modification," is written and used for minor changes. It is kept with the will and, again, your signature is witnessed. If major changes are desired, the estate plan should be updated or rewritten, and a new will prepared.

Selecting an Executor

An executor or executrix may be nominated in a will. The executor is responsible for the administration of the estate—paying valid debts and taxes, organizing assets, and distributing assets to beneficiaries. If there is no valid will, the court appoints an *administrator* or *administratrix.*

There is no single formula for choosing an executor. Each person has his or her own requirements—trust, administrative skills, familiarity with desires. Many persons name their spouse to serve as executor/executrix; others choose a child or close relative. The important thing is that the executor be competent and able to understand and follow prescribed requirements.

The executor named in a will does not have to serve and can decline the appointment. He may be unable to serve because of illness, injury, or absence from the country. It is important to name an alternate executor should the first named be unable to serve.

Selecting a Guardian for Minor Children

One of the most important choices made in a will is the nomination of a guardian for minor children in the event the death of both parents is simultaneous. A surviving natural or adoptive parent will be the guardian of the children unless he or she is proved unfit. The guardian usually has care and custody both of the minor children and of the property. In caring for the property, the **guardian** will:

* assume possession of the minor's property
* pay expenses of the guardianship
* prudently invest the minor's assets
* use funds for the maintenance and support of the minor under the supervision of the court
* account to the court as required from time to time
* file returns and pay taxes for the minor
* distribute the *corpus* and accumulated income of the guardianship when the minor reaches the age of majority

It is likely that the choice of guardian will be carefully examined by the court. If the guardian of the child and guardian of the property are not the same person, it is wise to find individuals who are compatible and on good terms. Sometimes, it is good to avoid a marked difference between the standard of living of the guardian and the child's available resources.

Guardians are entitled to a commission under state law. This is usually a percentage of receipts and disbursements.

Providing Cash for Estate Administration

It is important to plan so that adequate cash is available to an estate to assure the payment of administration expenses, federal and state income taxes, federal estate taxes, state *inheritance* or *estate taxes,* and other expenses, including any cash bequests.

Without planning, there could be serious complications. Most assets—farm, business, home, etc.—are not liquid and cannot easily be converted to cash without loss. One or more of the following **options** could be used in planning for cash in estate settlement:

* extension of time for paying federal estate taxes
* stock redemptions
* buy/out agreement between co-owners of a business
* sale of business assets during lifetime or at death
* accumulation of cash reserve
* life insurance

You will want to discuss these options with your attorney.

Postmortem Planning

Estate planning occurs during life to protect the estate and allow the best financial benefit for family and charities. Sometimes planning must occur after death, as well, to allow the goals to be met. Among the decisions: whether to elect alternate valuation date for federal estate taxes; whether a joint income tax return should be filed; whether to waive commission if spouse is executor; whether all of the marital deduction should be used; and whether disclaimers should be made for gift and estate tax estate-planning purposes. You should ask your attorney to explain these options available upon death.

Organizing the Plan

In planning your estate you will gather the necessary information, records, and documents for a conference with your attorney. You will need:

* family information
* existing wills—yours and your spouse's
* income tax returns for the last three years
* any gift tax returns filed
* life insurance policies of both spouses and children
* pension, profit-sharing, and deferred compensation plans
* business agreements relating to interests in corporations, partnerships, and sole proprietorships

* trust agreements
* buy/sell stock redemption agreements
* pre/postnuptial agreements
* titles of *joint tenancies* or *tenancies by the entireties*

The form "Preparing for an Estate-planning Conference with Your Attorney" will help you gather the necessary information for an estate-planning conference.

Letter of Last Instructions

You may wish to write a **letter of last instructions** to your surviving spouse or another person. This allows you to communicate, in an informal and loving way, helpful information or specific instructions. This letter is not legally binding, as a will is meant to be, but can be of great help.

This letter would contain any personal expressions to your surviving spouse and give a summary of information needed upon your death:

* location of your will, safe-deposit boxes, important papers, and records (chapter 12 contains forms for recording this information)
* names and addresses of persons to help surviving spouse (the form "Key Advisors" may serve as a guide)
* names, addresses, and telephone numbers of persons to be notified of your death ("Persons to Notify upon Death" may serve as a guide)
* funeral and burial instructions

Your surviving spouse may have all or much of this information already. This letter is intended to be a loving farewell and personal reminder. If you write a letter of last instructions, be sure it is easily located upon death. It should be kept at home, rather than in a safe-deposit box. If you wish the letter to remain sealed until death, you should leave it at your attorney's office.

II. Property and How It Is Owned

Ownership of Property

Of immense importance in estate planning is how both *real* and *personal property* are owned. You will need to know what property exists, where it is located, when you obtained it, what it cost, who paid for it, and if it was a gift or *inheritance*. Only then can you consider revisions in ownership to improve your plan.

You may need to search bank records, deeds, titles, bonds, and securities to determine if the property is solely yours, your spouse's, jointly owned, or community property. If it is jointly owned, you must know the amount each owner contributed.

Kinds of Joint Ownership

Joint ownership is a form of ownership where the entire property passes to the survivor upon the death of a joint tenant. It is wrong to assume that all property owned by husband and wife is jointly held by them. Jointly owned property is property owned by tenants specifically titled "joint tenants" or "tenants by the entirety". The exception is in *community property* states where special rules apply.

Tenancy by the entirety. This is a form of joint ownership between husband and wife. At the death of either, the survivor is sole owner. This right of survivorship cannot be destroyed unless both consent to do so. This form of ownership usually applies to real property, although some states apply it to personal property.

Joint tenancy. This is a type of joint ownership not limited to husband and wife. There is right of survivorship, and any joint tenant can transfer his or her interest during lifetime.

Tenancy in common. This is another type of joint ownership not limited to husband and wife. There is no right of survivorship; only the proportionate interest will go to the heirs. Any of the co-owners may dispose of his or her interest during life or by will at death.

Community property. This type of ownership exists in eight community property states—Arizona, California, Idaho, Louisiana, Nevada, New Mexico, Texas, and Washington. Usually property that either or both spouses acquires during marriage is considered held in community with each owning a half interest. Property owned at the time of marriage, individually inherited, or purchased with individual funds remains separate after marriage. Whether the income from separate property remains separate or becomes community property depends on the particular state law. Community property remains such, even if the owner moves to a noncommunity property state. If you live in a community property state, these laws are very important in your planning.

Dangers of Joint Ownership

Many people have the false impression that joint ownership saves trouble and taxes. The opposite may be true. From an estate-planning point of view, tenancy by the entirety and joint tenancy are not advisable. They can create problems for small estates as well as large ones. Joint ownership may prevent flexibility in estate planning.

D
A   * The right of survivorship precludes passing property by will, which might be
        preferred.
N   * Loss of full control, which might be needed.
G   * Sharing of income, which may present unfavorable tax consequences.
E   * Prevents planning at death, when options may be needed.
R   * Termination if divorce occurs, which is most difficult.
S

The Economic Recovery Tax Act of 1981 provides (for property jointly owned with the right of survivorship by spouses) that one-half of the property's value be included in the estate of the first to die. This applies regardless of the amount either spouse contributed toward purchase of the property.

The one-half property goes into the estate of the decedent at a "stepped up" basis, or current value. The one-half property of the surviving spouse keeps the old basis and may show a capital gain, which would be taxable. If property is solely held, it passes tax free to the surviving spouse at the higher basis.

Joint ownership is never a substitute for an estate or a will. Many estate-planning professionals recommend that the only property held jointly be the personal residence and a bank account. You should check this with your attorney.

CAUTION: How property is owned and the consequences of joint ownership are most important. Use the forms in chapter 12 to help gather the information needed for your attorney in planning the best way to own your property.

III. Taxes and the Transfer of Property

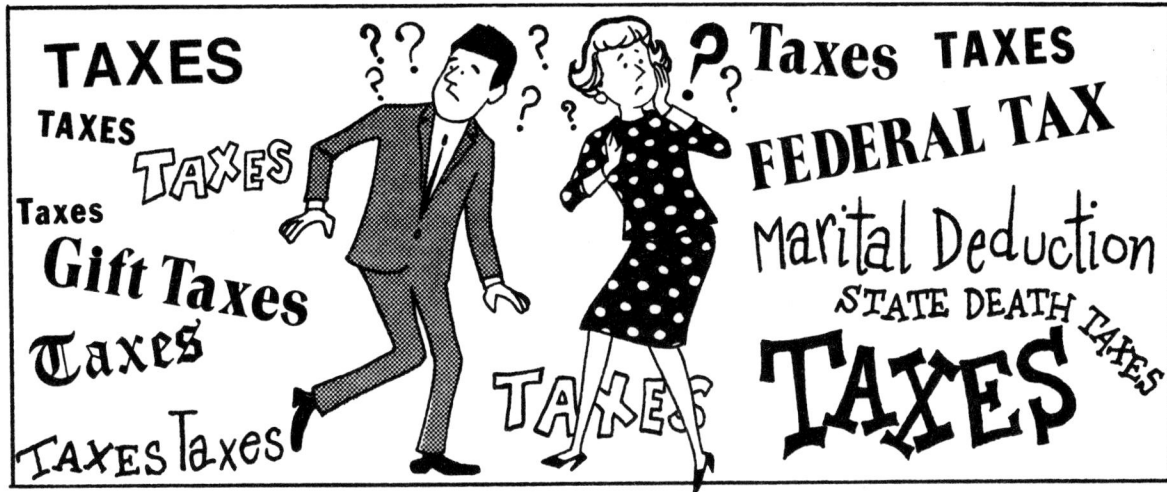

Certain taxes must be considered in estate planning. Understanding the tax laws will enable you to reduce your tax obligations and provide more for your family, other beneficiaries, and charities about which you are deeply concerned. If saving on taxes does not do a disservice to your beneficiaries or your beliefs, it is certainly justified. The Christian should always seek a balance between what is the best decision both from a business standpoint and from a human need and Christian ministry standpoint. They may or may not be the same.

Kinds of Taxes Related to Estate Planning

Persons doing estate planning must consider the following **taxes:**

* federal estate taxes
* state inheritance or estate taxes
* gift taxes
* federal income taxes
* state income taxes

The estate tax is imposed by the federal or state government on the right of the deceased to retain wealth at death. It is measured by the size of the taxable estate. An inheritance tax is assessed by some states on the right of receiving property from a decedent. It is imposed on the share of the estate that is distributed.

A gift tax is imposed by the federal government and by some states on the transfer of property by gift. No tax is imposed on gifts of $10,000 given annually to any number of persons ($20,000 if given with consent of spouse). This is called the annual exclusion (the Economic Recovery Tax Act of 1981 increased the annual exclusion from $3,000 to $10,000).

The Unified Credit Against Federal Estate and Gift Taxes

The unified credit is subtracted from the estate and gift tax liability, reducing the latter dollar for dollar. The credit when used during lifetime to offset gift taxes will reduce the available credit at time of death. Lifetime transfer and transfer at death are accumulated to determine the tax rate at death.

The Economic Recovery Tax Act of 1981 provides for a gradual increase of the unified credit against estate and gift taxes from $47,000 to $192,800 over a six-year period (the phase-in began January 1, 1982; for the amounts of the credit and its equivalent exemptions, see the table "Unified Credit Against Federal Estate and Gift Taxes"). This means that estates of persons dying in 1987 and in later years will have $600,000 exempt from federal estate and gift taxes; this is because the $192,800 unified credit is equivalent to a $600,000 exemption.

Example: $600,000 taxable estate in 1987

Tax on $500,000	$155,800
Tax on $100,000	37,000
Tax owed	$192,800
Less unified credit	$192,800
Tax due	-0-

Persons having an adjusted gross estate of $225,000 in 1982 will have no federal estate tax, because the unified credit will be equivalent to an exemption of that amount. Allowing for a 15 percent annual increase, an estate of that size will stay under the increased equivalent exemption and have no federal estate and gift tax obligation until 1990, when the estate value reaches $688,280; then a tax of $32,663.60 will be due.

Example: Adjusted gross estate of $688,280 in 1990

Tax on $500,000	$155,800.00
Tax on 188,280	69,663.60
Tax owed	$225,463.60
Less unified credit	192,800.00
Tax due	$ 32,663.60

Federal Estate and Gift Tax Rates

Prior to January 1, 1982, the maximum estate and gift tax rate was 70 percent. The 1981 Tax Act reduced this to 50 percent for estates over $2,500,000 in 1985 and later years. This rate is reduced over a four-year period in 5 percent increments.

For estates of persons dying in 1982, the maximum rate is 65 percent.

Over $2,500,000 but not over $3,000,000.................... $1,025,800 plus 53 percent of excess

Over $3,000,000 but not over $3,500,000.................... $1,290,800 plus 57 percent of excess

Over $3,500,000 but not over $4,000,000.................... $1,575,800 plus 61 percent of excess

Over $4,000,000.. $1,880,800 plus 65 percent of excess

For estates of persons dying in 1983, the maximum rate is 60 percent.

Over $3,500,000.. $1,575,800 plus 60 percent of excess

For estates of persons dying in 1984, the maximum rate is 55 percent.

Over $3,000,000.. $1,290,800 plus 55 percent of excess

For estates of persons dying in 1985, the maximum rate is 50 percent.

Over $2,500,000.. $1,025,000 plus 50 percent of excess

In 1985 and subsequent years, estates will be taxed at a uniform estate and gift tax rate from 18 to a maximum of 50 percent (see the table "Federal Estate and Gift Tax Rates"). Inflation and growth of the average taxable estate may prompt Congress to increase the unified credit or again reduce the maximum estate and gift tax rate.

State Death Taxes

The rules and rates for state death taxes vary. You may obtain them by contacting your attorney or the appropriate revenue office in your city or state capital.

The Marital Deduction

If you are married and want your spouse to receive all or part of your property, you may use the marital deduction. The 1981 Tax Act removed all quantitative limits on both the estate tax and gift tax marital deductions effective January 1, 1982. It also provides that certain *qualified terminable interests* are allowed these deductions. The unlimited marital deduction means that married persons may pass all or part of an estate to a spouse free of federal estate tax on the estate of the first spouse to die. And, it means that unlimited lifetime gifts may be made to a spouse free of federal gift taxes.

Should you use the marital deduction? That depends on your particular situation and the goals you wish to accomplish. The marital deduction does not have to be used. Estate planning for married persons concerns both lives, the first to die and the second to die. The question must always be asked, What will the benefit of the marital deduction be to the estate of the surviving spouse? Sometimes making maximum use of the unified credit will produce greater flexibility and tax savings than using the marital deduction.

If your estate plan was completed before January 1982, you may have a will with a maximum marital deduction clause. It is important to review and update your plan to assure it qualifies for the current unlimited marital deduction. Then again, you may find it better to eliminate use of this deduction.

CAUTION: Many of the rules relating to use of the marital deduction are technical and detailed. The phase-in of the unified credit could vary your need for and use of the marital deduction from year to year until 1987. Before deciding to use it, you need to plan carefully with the help of a competent attorney.

IV. Estimating the Federal Taxable Estate

Assets and Liabilities

You will need to know what you own and what you owe. Full disclosure of all assets and liabilities is essential. Never hide information from your attorney; you would only hurt yourself. You help yourself, your family, and other heirs when you reveal all the facts.

You will need to list all property and assets owned by you and your spouse and the kind of ownership. (The date property was obtained and the cost basis may be important later. Persons would do well to record this information. Again, the forms in chapter 12 may be used.) Life insurance, pensions, and annuities should be included. Chapter twelve contains forms to record this information and to discover your net worth.

Estimating the Federal Taxable Estate

You may estimate the federal taxable estate by listing all items included in the gross estate and deducting appropriate expenses, charitable contributions, deductions, and exclusions. The following items are included in the **gross estate:**

    I. All property—real or personal, tangible or intangible—in which you have an interest
    II. Value of property you transferred during life when:
        a. transfer of life insurance policies occurs within three years of death
        b. income is retained by you for life or for a period not determinable without reference to death
        c. transfer is intended to take effect at death
        d. the right to alter, amend, or revoke is retained
        e. any of the rights in *b, c,* and *d* are surrendered within three years of death
    III. One-half value of property with right of survivorship held jointly between spouses
    IV. The entire value of jointly held property between non-spouses unless survivor can prove he or she contributed to the purchase
    V. Life insurance proceeds if you have any incident of ownership or if proceeds are paid to executor or estate

VI. Property over which you have been given a general power of appointment

VII. Value of annuities

The following appropriate items are deductible from your gross estate to determine your adjusted gross estate, or **federal taxable estate:**

* funeral expenses
* administration expenses
* legal debts against the estate
* casualty losses not covered by insurance which may occur during administration
* mortgages and liens that are unpaid
* chariable contributions—for religious, educational, public institutions, government
* marital deduction for property transferred to surviving spouse (unlimited)
* $100,000 aggregate for certain qualified retirement plans

In estimating your federal taxable estate, you can only guess at some of the information. But it is only an estimate. An unexpected windfall or large settlement following an accidental death could cause a dramatic increase in the value of your estate or that of your spouse. Estate planning should consider this possibility.

You may use the form "Estimating Your Federal Taxable Estate." Then use the "Federal Estate and Gift Tax Rates" table to estimate your federal estate tax obligation. State inheritance and estate taxes vary. You should check with your attorney or the appropriate revenue office in your state.

Remember, if you are married, estate planning is always on both lives. Property transferred to the surviving spouse must be considered. You should estimate your federal taxable estate in two ways: (*a*) if you are the first to die and (*b*) if you are the surviving spouse.

NOTE: For estates of persons who die after December 31, 1982, the Tax Equity and Fiscal Responsibility Act of 1982 places a $100,000 limit on estate tax exclusion for retirement benefits under certain qualified retirement plans, IRAs, tax-sheltered annuities, and some military retirement plans. Use of the unified estate and gift tax credit, the marital deduction, and the charitable deduction would eliminate the tax in many estates. Persons with pension and retirement plans that might be affected by this limitation should check with a competent tax attorney.

V. Planning with Life Insurance

Life Insurance and Estate Planning

Life insurance is generally part of an effective estate plan. For this reason, it is important to have a life insurance agent on your estate-planning team. An insurance person who has reached the highest level of competency and qualifies by passing demanding examinations is designated Chartered Life Underwriter (CLU). A CLU has the knowledge and skill to incorporate life insurance into an estate plan in order to meet particular goals.

Life insurance may be used to replace earnings of family breadwinners and provide cash for settling an estate. Many families have two main breadwinners; planning should include both.

Insurance proceeds are exempt from federal estate taxes if they are payable to beneficiaries other than the executor or the estate and if no *incidents of ownership* are retained.

In estate planning you should consider **three important questions** about life insurance:

* On whom should new policies be taken out and how long should they be kept?
* Should any existing policy be removed from the gross estate by transferring ownership to another person?
* How should life insurance policies on other persons be kept out of the gross estate of the insured?

Kinds of Life Insurance

There are various kinds of life insurance which may be used for different purposes. The kinds, key points, and key uses follow:

Kind	Key Points	Key Uses
Whole Life	Premiums paid for life. Cost low. Builds cash value.	Offers young singles and marrieds protection with some savings.

Limited Payment Life	Premiums paid for a limited period. Protection stays in force when paid up. Builds cash value.	For short-term high income persons and midyear high income persons.
Single Premium Life	Protection minimal. Builds tax-free investment.	For persons in high tax bracket who want tax-free buildup and tax-free transfer of estate.
Endowment	Planned savings using declining term insurance as protection.	Forced savings plan for singles and persons building educational funds.
Term	Pure protection. Cost low.	For young marrieds with growing children who require large protection for a short period.
Reducing Term	Protection that reduces with time.	For protection of mortgages and other loans.
Survivorship Whole Life	Policy on two lives. Pays on second death. Guaranteed cash and paid-up insurance values.	With spouse or business co-owner to provide cash for payment of death taxes or business obligations.

Insurance for the Payment of Federal Estate Taxes

The phase-in of a lower maximum estate and gift tax rate and the increased unified credit against estate and gift taxes call for a careful revaluation of insurance needs yearly through 1987 for the payment of federal estate taxes. Unless your estate is over $600,000 in 1987 and later years and all the unified credit is available, you will pay no federal estate tax. If this size estate were passed to a surviving spouse with an estate of equal size, the federal estate tax would be $400,600 when the surviving spouse died. If the full unified credit of $192,800 were available, the tax due would be $207,800.

Careful planning for the payment of federal estate and gift taxes on the estate of the second to die is important. The use of survivorship whole life insurance, which pays only on the second death, should be considered. It has unique estate-planning uses, including guaranteed cash value which increases rapidly after the first death.

A two-life charitable gift annuity could be used in combination with survivorship whole life insurance. The after-tax portion of the annuity's guaranteed annual income would be used to purchase the policy (see "Asset Replenishment with a Gift Annuity").

Choosing the Beneficiary

When the insured is the policy owner, there are three options in the **choice of beneficiary:**

* executor/administrator
* other beneficiary (spouse, child, etc.)
* a trust

It is usually better to choose other beneficiaries or a trust than the executor. The consequences of your choice should be discussed with your attorney and a competent life insurance agent.

Settlement Options

There are **four settlement options** life insurance owners may use to spread out payment rather than taking the proceeds in a lump sum.

* Interest—Interest is paid for a limited period, then another option may be selected. A surviving spouse with young children might use this option while receiving social security benefits, then choose another option when this income ends.
* Fixed Period—Proceeds are paid over a fixed period in equal installments with fixed interest rate.
* Fixed Income—Proceeds are paid in fixed dollar amounts for a period of time, with the balance payable under another option.
* Life Income—An annuity is paid for life. There are three types: for the annuitant's life; for life, but with a number of installments guaranteed; and refund—if the annuitant dies before receiving the principal, the balance goes to a second beneficiary.

Insurance for a Wife

It has been wrongly assumed that life insurance should be on the breadwinning husband and the wife only needs insurance to cover burial expenses. Certainly the wife would benefit most if nearly all the insurance were on her husband, for he is likely to predecease her by seven to nine years.

Husbands are the real victims of noninsurance on the wife. Today in many homes, the wife is also an important breadwinner, and the family needs to consider adequate protection of that potential economic loss. Then, consider the economic value on the work done at home and see how high it is. In addition to the loss as wife, mother, and housekeeper, there would be loss of income splitting and use of the marital deduction. Another important reason for a wife's having adequate insurance is the need of cash for payment of taxes on, the administrative expenses of, her estate. "Key women" insurance is available for wives who are related to the family business.

Reviewing the Life Insurance Program

When **reviewing** the life insurance program, consider the following:

* needs of dependents
* insurance needed to increase estate size and which will support family if death should occur immediately
* availability of other assets
* pension and profit-sharing plans
* possible future inheritances

* kinds of insurance and cost
* age of the insured
* state law related to any death tax exemption of policy, if payable to a designated beneficiary
* credit life insurance to protect mortgages and debts
* cash value of present and future insurance policies
* use of waive-of-premium rider
* importance of health and accident insurance

CAUTION: Insurance needs vary. Probably the greatest need exists while children are growing up. As families change, insurance needs change; competent help should be sought from a life insurance agent. An attorney should advise you of the effect any insurance decision has on your estate plan.

VI. Gifts During Lifetime

Estate planning may include the transfer of wealth during life as well as at death. Persons may give personal property, real estate, life insurance, and annuities as lifetime gifts. Those who are considering such gifts should explore personal goals relating to them and the resulting tax consequences.

Personal Goals

Personal goals are more important than estate tax and income tax savings. You should not give away something if you really cannot afford to do so. Christian persons should determine the balance between motivation for good business and motivation to fulfill Christian responsibility. When persons who give are motivated primarily by benevolence, then tax consequences and estate-planning considerations should assume importance. The goal is to minimize income, estate, and gift taxes or have no tax at all related to the gift.

The Annual Exclusion

The Economic Recovery Tax Act of 1981 raised the annual exclusion from $3,000 to $10,000. This means that you may give $10,000 annually to as many persons as you wish without paying a federal gift tax. You need not file a gift tax form (required annually for larger gifts). If your spouse joins in making the gift, $20,000 is excluded. However, you are required to file a gift tax form, even though no tax is assessed.

Outright gifts of $10,000 or less usually present no problem to the donor. It is the gift of *future interest* that creates difficulties. Future interest is any interest in which possession or enjoyment begins at some future time. The annual exclusion is not available for future interest gifts.

The Marital Deduction

The 1981 Tax Act provides an unlimited marital deduction for lifetime gifts to a spouse. Also, it provides that certain terminable interests may qualify for this deduction. A qualified terminable interest means property that passes from the decedent and in which the spouse is entitled to all income for life.

To qualify, the property is treated as transferred to the donee-spouse, and no part is considered as retained by the donor or transferred to another person. An election to have such property qualify for the gift tax marital deduction must be made on the gift tax return for the calendar year the interest was transferred. Once the election is made, it is irrevocable.

There is a special rule for transfer of interests to a spouse and qualified charity for charitable remainder annuity trusts and unitrusts (although annuity and unitrust are specifically named, it is believed that a tax correction act may amend this to include any charitable remainder gift, which would include pooled income funds and gift annuities). The entire value will qualify for the marital deduction, and the spouse's estate for a charitable deduction. The donor receives an income tax charitable contribution deduction for the value of the remainder interest and a marital deduction for the value of the annuity or unitrust. No federal estate tax is imposed. This makes the annuity or unitrust an effective estate-planning tool. You should ask your attorney about its use.

To what extent should the marital deduction be used? Overuse may have serious tax consequences on the estate of the surviving spouse. Never assume that all lifetime gifts should be made under the marital deduction. Taxwise, it may be better to balance use of the marital deduction with the unified credit against estate and gift taxes. Under this provision, in 1987 and later years $600,000 may be given tax free.

In addition to using the unified credit, a testamentary trust naming the surviving spouse as beneficiary with remainder to the children would keep property out of the surviving spouse's estate. A charitable remainder trust could also be used to accomplish this.

Kinds of Gifts

Gifts Between Spouses. The unlimited lifetime marital gift tax deduction means that persons may give any amount to a spouse during life without a federal gift tax (a number of states impose a gift tax; this should be considered when planning lifetime gifts). You are limited only by personal goals and good estate-planning practices. As mentioned earlier, unplanned use of the marital deduction could have serious tax consequences later. When considering lifetime gifts to a spouse, you should consult your attorney.

Gifts to Minors. Gifts from parents to children, and grandparents to grandchildren are the most common lifetime gifts. If the gift is small, there is no concern for tax consequences. Tax and legal matters become important as the size of the gift increases.

State law is concerned with the legal capacity of a minor to own and care for property. Trusts, custodianships, and guardianships are vehicles for gifts to minors and help protect their interests.

The Uniform Gift to Minors Act, adopted in most states, provides for the transfer of property to minors. It allows a legal custodian to act without guardianship.

Split Gift. When a married person makes a gift to a child, grandchild, parent, or any third party, the gift (for gift tax purposes) may be treated as though one-half is made by donor and one-half is made by spouse if spouse consents. The gift is split for computing the gift tax at a lower rate than it would have been taxed as a single gift.

Example: The gift tax on a $100,000 gift is $23,800. On two gifts of $50,000 each, it is $21,200—a savings of $2,600.

Gifts in Contemplation of Death. Gifts made within three years of death are no longer considered given in contemplation of death and are not included in the estate of the donor. There are exceptions: property used for determining qualification for special use valuation, deferral of estate taxes, and stock redemption for a farm or closely held business.

A Continuing Program of Lifetime Gifts. A continuing program of lifetime gifts using all or part of the annual exclusion is one way to reduce estate taxes without gift tax costs. This usually begins when parents have reached the life stage when needs are less and survivors will be adequately provided for with one-half of the then-current estate. Charitable remainder trusts, pooled income funds, and gift annuities are effective estate-planning vehicles in a program of lifetime gifts.

Income Tax Savings Related to Lifetime Gifts

It is possible to save on income tax by spreading ownership of property among family members. **Gifts of appreciated property:**

* Donor holding highly appreciated property may wish to sell it for investment purposes but does not because of high capital gain. A gift of this property to a low-tax-bracket family member will reduce the cost of the gift.
* There is no gift, no income splitting, and no gift tax unless the gift is complete.

The Federal Gift Tax

The federal gift tax applies to all gifts over $10,000 ($20,000 if given jointly with spouse). The tax applies both to direct and indirect gifts. A direct gift may create a trust, forgive a debt, assign insurance benefits, or give cash, bonds, or certificates of deposit.

Indirect gifts may include paying the expenses of someone (except when there is legal obligation to do so) or making a gift to someone for the benefit of another.

The Economic Recovery Tax Act of 1981 provides an unlimited gift tax exclusion for certain transfers for educational and medical expenses. A qualified transfer would be any amount paid on behalf of an individual as tuition to an educational institution for education or training. Also allowed are transfers as payment to any person who provides medical care for an individual.

If the sale of appreciated property is necessary to meet certain family expenses, such as college education for a child or grandchild, it may be advisable to transfer the property to that family member as a gift and let him or her sell it. The gain would be taxed in the lower bracket of the child.

Payment of the Federal Gift Tax

The 1981 Tax Act provides that all federal gift tax returns be filed and any gift tax paid on an annual basis. A gift tax return must be filed when a gift exceeds $10,000, whether a tax is due or not. The Unified Estate and Gift Tax Rate applies, as does the lifetime credit. The tax is paid by the donor.

Timing of Gifts

If gifts of securities are made, low points in the market will maximize the gifts and minimize gift tax or credit costs. There is no carry-over for unused annual exclusion when giving at the end of the year.

CAUTION: Since some states impose a gift tax, it is important to know state law. You will want to check if your state imposes a tax on lifetime gifts. These gifts should be planned. Always check the consequences of such gifts with your attorney before making them.

VII. Planning Charitable Giving

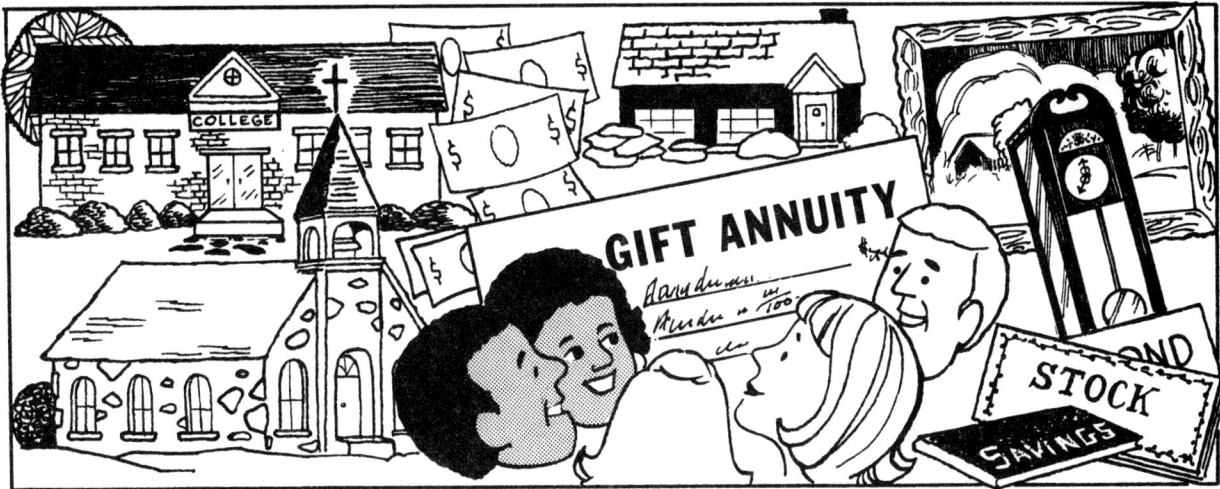

American Voluntarism

Since colonial days, Americans have been a giving people—from simply helping a neighbor to building churches, hospitals, and educational institutions. The government has recognized the importance of voluntary contributions to the quality of life in our nation. Tax advantages for charitable giving were built into the American system to encourage support of worthwhile causes. The principal is not to tax income that is given away rather than consumed. Using these benefits will enable you to give more. Persons should not give just to save on taxes. On the other hand, giving without understanding the tax advantages is poor Christian stewardship.

Rules for Non-itemizers

Until recently, only taxpayers who itemized deductions were allowed a deduction for charitable contributions. The Economic Recovery Tax Act of 1981 allows non-itemizers—those who use the Zero Bracket Amount (ZBA), formally called standard deduction—to deduct charitable gifts beginning January 1, 1982. This direct charitable deduction will be phased in over a period of five years.

For married taxpayers filing joint returns and for single taxpayers in 1982 and 1983, 25 percent of the first $100 of charitable gifts will be deductible—a limit of $25; for 1984, 25 percent of the first $300 will be deductible—a limit of $75.

For married taxpayers filing separately, the limit is one-half the applicable amount—$50 in 1982-83 and $150 in 1984.

In 1985, 50 percent of *all* charitable gifts may be deducted; and in 1986, 100 percent will be deductible.

New regulations provide substantiation requirements for those claiming this deduction. By 1986, it is expected that non-itemizers will give over $6 billion annually in charitable contributions. The direct charitable deduction for non-itemizers is scheduled to end December 31, 1986, unless reenacted by Congress.

Kinds of Giving

Stewardship of accumulating resources makes it possible to strengthen the work of Christ now and continue it in the future, even after a person's death.

Remember that charitable contributions are deductible in the year payment is made.

Gifts of cash. These gifts are deductible up to 50 percent of adjusted income (the contribution base is adjusted income without net operating loss [Internal Revenue Code § 170 (d)]). Five additional years are allowed to carry over any excess above this 50 percent.

Securities and real estate that have appreciated in value. These, when held a year or more, are deductible at the present fair market value rather than the lower cost basis. In addition, there is no capital gain on the appreciation. These gifts are deductible up to 30 percent of adjusted income with five-year carry-over for any excess. If held less than a year, the deduction is at cost basis.

Securities now worth less. You may sell and give proceeds—thus deduct the gift and take a capital loss on your tax return.

Bargain sales of securities or real estate. The charitable contribution is the difference between the bargain sale price and the actual fair market value. There is no capital gain on the gift part.

Tangible personal property. Works of art, antiques, coins, etc. are deductible at the current fair market value rather than the cost basis if held a year or more. There is no capital gain tax on appreciation when the gift is used for the charity's exempt purpose (e.g., painting given to an art museum). The gift is deductible up to 30 percent of the adjusted income with five-year carry-over for any excess. If held less than a year, the deduction is at cost basis.

Crops and inventories. Other ordinary income property is deductible at the cost basis up to 50 percent of adjusted income with five-year carry-over for any excess.

Corporate gifts. These gifts may be deductible up to 10 percent of corporation's taxable income with five-year carry-over for any excess.

Gifts of scientific property used for research. These may be deducted equal to the cost basis plus 50 percent of appreciation for qualified corporate contributions when made to a college or university for research. The gift must be given within two years of construction.

Partnership gifts. These gifts are deductible on individual tax returns, not partnership returns.

Farms or personal residences. These may be given while retaining the right to live on or use the property for life (and the life of a spouse or other person, if desired). An income tax contribution deduction is available the year the gift is made based on the value of the remainder interest determined by using Treasury tables.

Life insurance. You can irrevocably assign incidents of ownership to a charity. A gift of *paid up policy* generally provides a deduction of replacement cost. A policy with *premiums still to be paid* yields a deduction that is approximately the present cash surrender value. In addition, premiums are deducted annually. *New policy* premiums are deducted annually.

Gifts that pay an income for life. You may give cash, securities, or real property in trust to a church or other charitable institution with the provision that the income be received for life and, if you desire, the life of a spouse or other person. An income tax charitable contribution deduction is available the year the gift is made. This contribution deduction is not for the entire amount but is based on the gift's remainder interest, your age, and the percentage of income you will receive. Since the asset is removed from your estate, there is no federal estate tax on its value.

These life income agreement gifts are: charitable remainder trusts, pooled income funds, and gift annuities. They provide an opportunity to benefit a worthwhile charity while protecting your family with an income for life. Upon death, the remainder of the gift becomes the property of the designated charity. These life income gifts have a variety of estate-planning uses, and when creating them, care should be taken that all regulations and requirements are met. You will want to discuss this with your advisors.

Charitable Remainder Unitrust. You or beneficiary receives an annual fixed percentage of income for life (minimum is 5 percent) of net fair market value of trust assets calculated annually. There is no capital gains tax when appreciated securities are used to fund the unitrust. The income you receive is taxed as ordinary income or as a capital gain or is tax exempt when applicable.

A *net income unitrust* pays net income earned not exceeding the trust instrument. The *net income plus make-up unitrust* allows for make-up in future years when income exceeds stated percentage if there was any shortage in previous annual payments.

Example: John Donor, age fifty-five, transfers $10,000 to a 6 percent unitrust and receives a $600 income the first year. If the unitrust is valued at $12,000 the next year, he receives $720. The income may fluctuate year to year based on the trust's value. John receives an income tax charitable contribution deduction of $3,822 the year the unitrust is funded. If Jane Donor, same age, makes the same gift, her contribution deduction is $3,014. It is less than John's, because her life expectancy is longer and she has use of the income for more years. Every additional $10,000 added later will provide a contribution deduction based on John's or Jane's age at that time.

Charitable Remainder Annuity Trust. You or beneficiary receives fixed dollar payments annually. The minimum amount is 5 percent of the initial fair market value of the trust property. There is no capital gains tax when the trust is funded with appreciated securities. The income is taxed the same as unitrusts.

Example: Jane Donor, age sixty-five, wishes to make a charitable gift and has determined she needs a $1,250 annual income in return. She funds an annuity trust with $25,000 to provide this amount. If the income is higher, the excess is reinvested in the trust. If lower, the deficit is paid from capital gains or from the principal. Jane receives an income tax charitable contribution deduction of $13,375 the year the gift is made. If John Donor, same age, makes this gift, he receives a contribution deduction of $14,956.

Pooled Income Funds. A pooled income fund is a trust created by a charity and funded by a number of donors who receive a pro rata share of the fund's earnings each year for life (and life of a secondary beneficiary, if desired). There is no capital gains tax when appreciated securities are transferred to the pooled fund. Earnings from the fund are taxed as ordinary income. The year the gift is made, official Treasury tables are used to calculate the income tax charitable contribution deduction, which is based on the donor's age and use of the pooled fund the remainder of life.

Example: John Donor, age sixty-one, transfers $10,000 in appreciated securities to a denominational pooled income fund, naming his wife, Jane, age fifty-five, as second beneficiary. If the pooled fund earns 9 percent, he receives $900 this year and will receive a share of whatever the fund earns each year for his life and Jane's. The income tax charitable contribution deduction is $2,496.90, which is based on their ages and the use of the pooled fund over a two-life term.

Gift Annuity. A gift annuity is part gift and part purchase of an annuity. You or beneficiary receives a guaranteed fixed dollar amount each year for life; a large portion is tax free. The annuity rate is determined by the Committee on Gift Annuities' actuarial tables. if appreciated securities are used to purchase the annuity, there is a capital gains tax on only part of the gift. This gain may be spread over the annuitant's life. Gift annuities may be on one or two lives. An income tax charitable contribution deduction is available the year the annuity is purchased, based on the annuitant's age, life expectancy, and amount of gift.

Example: Jane Donor, age seventy, purchases a $25,000 gift annuity to benefit her college. She receives a guaranteed income of 7.1 percent, or $1,775 each year for life, of which $1,169.00 is tax free. Her contribution deduction is calculated to be $8,048.75. If John Donor, age seventy-six, purchased this same annuity, he would receive an income of 8.1 percent, or $2,025, of which $1,518.75 is tax free. His contribution deduction would be $11,940. A two-life annuity for John and Jane Donor would provide an annual income of 6.6 percent, or $1,650.00, of which $1,056.00 is tax free. The contribution deduction would be $7,680.00.

Deferred Payment Gift Annuity. The deferred payment gift annuity allows you to make a charitable gift now with the purchase of an annuity but defer the annual annuity income until later, perhaps retirement. The annual income will be based on your age at the time payment begins, as will your charitable contribution deduction.

Example: John Donor, age fifty, purchases a $50,000 gift annuity to benefit his church, with annual payments to begin at age sixty-five. At that age, he will receive an annual income of 11.0 percent, or $5,500.00, guaranteed each year for life, of which $1,380.00 is tax free. His charitable contribution deduction of $29,150.00 is based on age sixty-five but is available now at age fifty.

===================================★ ★ ★====================================

Asset Replenishment with a Gift Annuity. The gift annuity has been used as a vehicle to replenish estate assets. This concept, which was pioneered by the Joseph J. Brennan Agency, Inc., Spring Lake, New Jersey, has made larger gift annuities very attractive. The concept is simple.

A gift annuity is purchased, and the after-tax amount of the guaranteed annual income is given to heirs using the annual gift tax exclusion to make the gift. The heirs can use this gift to purchase the property of life insurance on the donor's life. This asset is owned by and payable to an irrevocable life insurance trust distributed to the heirs upon the donor's death. This trust must contain *Crummey* powers and should be drafted by a competent attorney. *Crummey* powers give the equivocal right to make withdrawals necessary to assure the gift tax exclusion. The gifted asset is "replenished" in the heirs' estate.

Example: John Donor, age sixty-five, would like to make a $100,000 gift to his church-related retirement home. He is also concerned that his children have adequate assets. He purchases a $100,000 gift annuity to benefit the retirement home and receives an income tax charitable contribution deduction of $35,069. His guaranteed annual income of $6,600, of which $4,475 is tax free, provides an after-tax income of $5,538 (if John is in the 50 percent tax bracket). This after-tax income is gifted to his children and is used to purchase $106,000 of whole life insurance on John's life which is placed in an irrevocable insurance trust payable to them. If John were age forty-five and made the same gift, he would replenish the $100,000 gifted asset with $220,000 of whole life insurance purchased with after-tax income. John has the joy of making a charitable gift, removing an asset from his taxable estate, and "replenishing" the asset for his children.

The unlimited federal estate and gift tax marital deduction is likely to result in substantial tax upon the estate of the second to die. To provide for heirs and to keep the estate from shrinking, the asset replenishment concept may be used with a two-life charitable gift annuity using survivorship whole life insurance, which pays only on the second death.

Example: John, age sixty-nine, and Jane, age sixty-three, purchase a $100,000 two-life gift annuity to benefit their church-related college and receive an income tax contribution deduction of $22,209. Their annual income is $6,200, of which $3,720 is tax free. Their after-tax income of $4,960 (if they are in the 50 percent tax bracket) is gifted to their children and used to purchase $164,500 of survivorship whole life insurance. This is placed in an irrevocable insurance trust containing *Crummey* powers with the children as beneficiaries. Guaranteed cash value increases rapidly, especially after the first death. John and Jane have the joy of making a substantial charitable gift and assuring that their estate will not be eroded following the second death.

★ ★ ★

Denominational Foundations

Denominational foundations provide an opportunity through which you may give to your local church or to denominational institutions, boards, agencies, or special ministries through immediate, life income or deferred gifts programs. These foundations can help donors and their advisors understand the tax advantages of various charitable gifts and are available to be part of an estate-planning team.

CAUTION: Charitable giving should be considered in any estate plan. For a Christian, it is natural to plan charitable gifts. The income tax, gift tax, and estate tax consequences of charitable gifts depend on the unique circumstances of each donor. When considering these gifts, donors should consult their advisors.

VIII. Use of Trusts

- PERSONAL TRUST
- TESTAMENTARY TRUST
- INTERVIVOS TRUST   - BENEFICIARIES

TRUST

Using Trusts in Estate Planning

A trust is a versatile estate-planning tool. It is an arrangement in which a person holds legal title for another and manages the affairs for the latter's benefit. A trust may be used to protect minors, manage property, and reduce taxes.

Trust Terminology

* *trustee:* one who holds legal title for another and manages the trust for that person's benefit
* *beneficiary:* one who benefits from a trust
* *settlor:* one who creates a trust—also called *creator, donor, grantor, trustor*
* *corpus:* property held by a trustee—sometimes called *principal* or *trust property*
* *trust agreement:* terms of a trust
* *inter vivos trust:* trust created during the settlor's lifetime
* *testamentary trust:* trust created in a will
* *fiduciary:* relationship of the trustee to the beneficiary; one who is accountable, prudent, and loyal

By carefully selecting a trustee, you can provide for the thorough management of property while relieving the beneficiary of that responsibility. If the trust is properly worded, it can meet the demands of any change that might occur and can be tailored to meet individual family needs.

Kinds of Trusts

The table on the following page outlines different kinds of trusts, their key features, key advantages, and key tax consequences.

How Trusts Are Taxed

Trusts are subject to income, gift, and estate taxes. Just how the trust is treated taxwise depends on the workings and purpose of its creation. Whether a trust should or should not be included in an estate is determined by each particular situation and the use intended by the creator.

CAUTION: The use of trusts in estate planning can be very helpful. Since the needs of families vary, the kinds of trusts necessary to meet estate-planning needs will also vary; persons should seek the guidance of a competent attorney.

Kind of Trust	Key Features	Key Advantages	Key Income Tax Consequences	Key Gift Tax Consequences	Key Estate Tax Consequences
Charitable Remainder	Irrevocable.	Provides income for one or two lives, then remainder goes to designated charity. Charitable contribution deduction for value of remainder interest.	Trust income taxable to donor. Sometimes capital gains tax may apply.	None.	None.
Clifford	Short-term. At least ten years or life of beneficiary; then corpus reverts to creator.	Income splitting to reduce income tax. Investment and control are supervised.	Taxable to beneficiary if current income is distributed. Capital gain or loss will be taxed currently to creator.	Tax on value of income interest. Annual exclusion applies.	Included in estate of creator.
Irrevocable	Cannot be revoked.	Avoids probate. Investment and control are supervised.	Taxable to beneficiary if current income is distributed. If income accumulates to trust, the trust will be taxed. If income accumulates first to trust, then to beneficiary on distribution, special throw-back rules may apply.	Taxable to creator. Annual exclusion is available for gifts of present interest.	Not taxable unless creator retains powers that would cause trust to be taxed in the estate.
Revocable	May be revoked.	Avoids probate. Investment and control are supervised.	Trust income taxable to creator.	None.	Included in estate of creator.
Testamentary	Created by will.	Investment and control are supervised.	Taxable to beneficiary if current income is distributed. If income accumulates to trust, the trust will be taxed. If income accumulates first to trust, then to beneficiary on distribution, special throw-back rules may apply.	None.	Included in estate of creator. Possible to avoid tax on death of beneficiary.

IX. Planning with Social Security

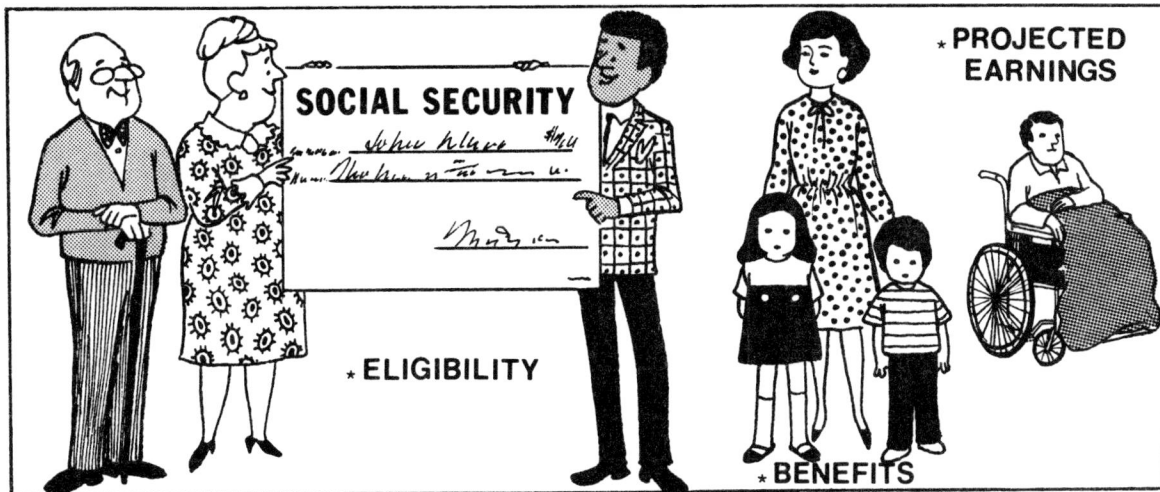

Social Security and Estate Planning

Social security is based on the concept that during working years persons pay a tax that is pooled in a separate trust fund and pays benefits during retirement, disability, and upon death. Part of the contribution goes into a separate Hospital Trust Fund that provides workers and dependents reaching age sixty-five with coverage of hospital bills.

Nine out of ten jobs are covered by social security; yet most persons are unaware of the benefits and have only a vague awareness that at age sixty-five some indeterminable income will start. Persons planning their estate should understand social security benefits, what protection is offered, and how the **benefits** can be integrated with a pension for retirement. For those covered by social security:

* retirement checks can start at age sixty-two
* workers severely disabled before sixty-five get disability checks
* survivors get monthly benefits
* persons reaching age sixty-five and those disabled earlier have hospital and medical insurance
* a death benefit of $255 is provided for a living-with surviving spouse or children under eighteen entitled to benefits

Eligibility

Before persons or family get social security benefits, eligibilty must be established based on a specified amount of work measured in "quarters of coverage."

Work Credit for Retirement Benefits	
If you reach 62 in	Years of employment you need
1979	7
1981	7½
1983	8
1987	9
1991 or later	10

Work Credit for Survivors and Disability Benefits

Born after 1929, die or become disabled at	Born before 1930, die or become disabled before 62 in	Years of employment you need
28 or younger		1½
30		2
32		2½
34		3
36		3½
38		4
40		4½
42		5
44		5½
46		6
48		6½
50	1979	7
52	1981	7½
54	1983	8
56	1985	8½
58	1987	9
60	1989	9½
62 or older	1991 or later	10

Earnings Record and Estimate of Benefits

To review your earnings record and get an estimate of benefits based on current and projected earnings, write:

> Social Security Administration
> P.O. Box 57
> Baltimore, MD 21203

You may use the card below (form SSA-7004 PC [1-79]), available at your local social security office, or request the same information in a letter.

(Please read instructions on back before completing)

REQUEST FOR SOCIAL SECURITY STATEMENT OF EARNINGS

Your social security number

Date of Birth

Month	Day	Year

Print Name and Address in ink or use typewriter

Please send a statement of my social security earnings to:

Name _____

Number & Street _____

City & State _____ Zip Code _____

Sign Your Name Here _____
(Do Not Print)

I am the individual to whom the record pertains. I understand that if I knowingly and willingly request or receive a record about an individual under false pretenses I would be guilty of a Federal crime and could be fined up to $5,000.

If you ever used a name (such as a maiden name) on a social security card different from the one above, please print name here:

_____

You will not get a detailed answer, but social security has an internal coding that will tell the computer to give a more detailed response. "QC" written at the bottom of the card will give the number of quarters credited to your account and show if you have worked enough for benefits. "Estimate" written there will tell the computer to estimate what benefits you might receive based on your current and projected earnings.

CAUTION: There is a statutory limit of 3 years, 3 months, and 15 days to correct your record of earnings. Therefore, persons should check earnings every 3 years.

HINT: Social Security welcomes questions by telephone, correspondence, or personal visit to the local office. They prefer, however, using the telephone for almost any type of business, including statement of earnings.

The Future of Social Security

Congress continues to review social security and find ways to keep it solvent. Recent changes relate to minimum benefits, earlier ending of widow-mother benefits, and the elimination of student benefits after a phase-out period.

More changes are likely. It is important to keep informed by regularly checking with your local social security office and with your advisor.

X. Estate Planning in Special Situations

The owner of a business, the owner of a farm or ranch, or a single woman, divorcée, or widow has a unique estate-planning situation.

For the Owner of a Business

Estate planning is part of **business planning.** A person who owns an interest in a business may find it is the largest asset in the estate. In planning the estate, it must be decided:

* if and how the business will continue
* the valuation of the business for tax purposes
* what personnel will manage the business—family or key business persons

The use of buy/sell agreements and stock redemption plans are effective estate-planning options for the business owner. They are used to assure the best disposition of a business, either continued by the family or sold to a partner or others.

Fixing the value of a business and business real estate is important. The Economic Recovery Tax Act of 1981 allows the fair market value of real property to be reduced resulting from current use valuation. The maximum amount by which the fair market value of qualified property may be reduced is $600,000 for estates of persons dying in 1981 (increased from the previous allowable amount of $500,000), $700,000 for estates of those dying in 1982, and $750,000 for 1983 and later years.

If you have a closely held business the value of which exceeds 35 percent of your adjusted gross estate or 50 percent of the federal taxable estate, a fourteen-year period for payment of federal estate taxes relating to business interest is possible. Interest only is paid the first four years, and the rate is 4 percent on the first $1 million.

A number of charitable giving plans, such as charitable remainder trusts and gift annuities, are effective estate-planning vehicles for the business owner.

CAUTION: A person who owns a business has a particular need for competent estate-planning help to protect both business and family. This kind of estate planning is well worth the cost.

For the Owner of a Farm or Ranch

Farmers and ranchers often want their children to continue the business. Taxes and the economics of **farming and ranching** make this very difficult without careful planning. Without liquid assets to settle the estate, paying federal estate taxes (which could be as high as 65 percent of the fair market value of the farm or ranch in 1982, 60 percent in 1983, 55 percent in 1984, and 50 percent in 1985 and later years) could be disastrous. It is most important to plan carefully with the help of competent advisors. You will want to consider finding a tax attorney who is experienced in these particular areas.

Among the things you must plan for are:

* minimizing federal and state death taxes
* providing the cash necessary for the farm or ranch to continue
* providing fairly for the heirs who remain in the business and for those who have left the farm or ranch

An executor may elect to **value the real property on its value as a farm or ranch,** rather than the fair market value on its highest and best use, such as development purposes. This special valuation cannot reduce the estate more than $750,000 for persons dying in 1983 and later ($700,000 for those dying in 1982). A number of rules apply.

* The decedent must have been a citizen or resident of the United States at death.
* The value of the farm or ranch, both real and personal property, must be at least 50 percent of the gross estate reduced by debts and expenses.
* At least 25 percent of the adjusted value of the gross estate must qualify as farm real property.
* The real property must pass to a qualifying heir.
* The real property must have been owned by the decedent or family member and used or held as a farm in five out of the eight years immediately preceding death.
* There must have been material participation in the farm operation by the decedent or family member in five of the last eight years immediately preceding the earliest of: the date of death, the date decedent became disabled, or decedent's retirement date. A surviving spouse will be considered as having materially participated during periods when the decedent actively managed the farm.
* The election must be made on the decedent's estate tax form. Once made, it is irrevocable.

A qualified heir is a member of the decedent's family which includes spouse, parents; brothers, sisters, children, stepchildren, and their spouses; and lineal descendants of these individuals.

A maximum period of fourteen years for installment payment of federal estate taxes may be elected if the farm business exceeds 35 percent of the adjusted gross estate. Only interest is paid the first four years at a special rate of 4 percent on the first $1 million. The balance is paid in ten annual installments of interest and principal.

The farm must continue in use by the qualified heir for a ten-year estate tax recapture period. There is a two-year grace period in which the qualified heir may commence the farm business without the recapture tax being imposed. Any part of the two-year grace period used will be added to the ten-year recapture period. A recapture tax will be imposed if the qualified heir fails to operate the farm business or ceases the farm business during the recapture period.

In providing for **heirs who have left the farm,** persons should consider:

* providing cash which if invested would give absentee heirs about as much as those operating the farm
* providing absentee heirs an interest in the farm or stock in the farm corporaton with an option to purchase at a fair price
* providing some way for the absentee heirs to participate in the farm profits as landlords, debtors, or security holders

Charitable giving can be very effective in any estate plan of a farmer or rancher. Gifts of land, crops, and livestock can be used to reduce tax liabilities. Charitable remainder trusts and charitable gift annuities are effective estate-planning vehicles. Gift of a farm or ranch while retaining a life estate for self and spouse might be useful for those intending to retire from the operation in the future.

Special Rules for Woodlands. The 1981 Tax Act continues the treatment of timber operations as a farming use but permits an executor to elect to specially value the standing timber. The recapture tax is imposed when the qualified heir cuts or disposes of the timber during the recapture period.

For a Single Woman, Divorcée, or Widow

A single woman, divorcée, or widow has unique estate-planning considerations. She has no marital deduction to use. She does, however, have use of the unified estate and gift tax credit (see the "Unified Credit Against Federal Estate and Gift Taxes" table). If she is a widow, she may have received from her deceased husband under the current unlimited marital deduction and now have a sizable estate which qualifies for federal estate taxes.

The single woman would do well to focus on lifetime objectives rather than on postdeath planning. If her estate now or in the future is large enough so that federal estate taxes would be paid, steps to reduce the estate should be considered. Charitable remainder trusts, pooled income funds, and gift annuities could be used to provide the single person with income for life with the remainder going to her church and other charities. Also, a life insurance program may be designed for a single woman to provide her estate with cash and to build a retirement fund.

To be sure, nothing (if it might be needed later) should be given away just to save a possible estate tax.

CAUTION: The single woman, divorcée, or widow should have the help of a competent advisor in planning her estate.

XI. Administering an Estate

Probate

Probate is the process of proving a will valid and administering an estate of a decedent. The will is statutory, and laws vary among states. The law calls for an executor—a person or a bank—to be responsible for organizing assets, paying funeral expenses, valid debts, and taxes, and distributing any remaining assets to beneficiaries or heirs.

If a will exists, it must be proven valid before an executor can be appointed (some states allow a *self-proving will* accompanied by an affadavit of witnesses at the time of the will's execution, making it unnecessary for them to appear when the will is probated). A family member or friend must locate the will and present it to the local probate court. A hearing date is set and notification given. Any arguments for or against the admission of the will may be heard. Witnesses will be present or later contacted to prove signatures are genuine. When the will is proven valid, the executor is appointed.

The executor named in the will may be appointed if he does not decline the appointment or is not declared unfit to serve. The executor must file a petition asking the court for appointment.

If for some reason the named executor cannot be appointed, a relative or friend may petition the court for appointment. When the court determines who will serve, letters testamentary are issued giving the executor authority to act.

In cases where no will exists or the will is not valid, the court will appoint a person or bank to serve as administrator. All states require the executor or administrator to post a bond with the court to protect the estate against dishonest administration. This bond is usually equal to the dollar value of the estate's assets. A will may state that the executor serve without posting bond.

Persons who are appointed executor or administrator may need the services of a competent attorney skilled in estate settlement.

Duties of the Executor

The first responsibility of an executor is the payment of valid debts. A notice is placed in a local newspaper to inform creditors that they must present valid proof of outstanding claims against the estate. If creditors fail to notify the executor within a time limit set by state law, the estate is not liable for the debt. Mortgages and other debts are of public record, and the executor must find them if there are any.

State law also gives a priority order for debt payment. If the assets are not sufficient, the executor will be personally liable for unpaid debts that have statutory preference.

Organizing Assets. Organizing assets is often slow and time consuming. It involves reviewing the decedent's records and locating safe-deposit boxes, bank accounts, real property, stocks and bonds, cars, boats, stamp and coin collections, and *all* other property. Checking and savings accounts and stocks and bonds must be reregistered in the executor's name. Tangible personal property (antiques, coins, clothing, jewelry, etc.) is not retitled to the executor but delivered by him to the beneficiary.

Payment of Taxes. The executor is responsible for the payment of any federal and state income taxes, the federal estate tax, and any state inheritance or estate taxes. The federal and state income taxes must be paid on the regular date due. The federal estate tax must be paid nine months following the date of death. State inheritance or estate taxes are payable according to state law.

The executor will need to know the various elections available in estate administration which will affect tax liabilities.

Administrative Expenses. The expenses related to administration—attorney's fees, appraisal fees, court filing fees, upkeep of real property—are paid from the estate. Providing cash for these expenses is part of estate planning (see "Providing Cash for Estate Administration").

Notifying Beneficiaries. An executor is responsible for notifying all beneficiaries. This is usually done in writing a short time after the executor is appointed. State law should be followed.

Accounting. The executor must prepare and file accountings of his fiduciary duties—death payment, expenses, taxes, holdings in and investment of decedent's property. State law may require that copies of this accounting go to beneficiaries who have the right to question or object to any part.

Distribution of Assets. The executor distributes the probate property to all beneficiaries. This is usually the last thing done. In fact, if the executor pays beneficiaries before debts, expenses, and taxes, he is personally liable for any deficit.

Executor's Commission

State law provides a commission for the work of an executor. This is a statutory amount, usually a percentage of estate assets or reasonable compensation interpreted by the court.

XII. Forms for Gathering Information

A Roadmap for Planning   Starring..... YOUR FAMILY

The forms that follow will be useful in gathering the information, documents, and records necessary to develop an effective estate plan. Records are a road map for planning. They tell you where you are and help you plan how best to get where you wish to go. The information you gather will be helpful in several ways.

To share with your attorney. Your attorney and estate-planning team will need accurate and complete information in order to maximize your estate plan.

To serve as a family record. Family records are important and should be preserved. Each family is unique, and records tell their story. You may wish to write a family history and attach a copy to your records.

To be updated from time to time. Family records should be updated when change affects the family: a new job promotion or educational attainment; moving or retiring; at times of celebration, a marriage, or a new baby; when death occurs. Review your records at least annually. Decide on a time. An anniversary or birthday may suit. Some may choose the week between Christmas and New Year's Day as a good time to update family records.

It is a lot of work; it takes time. Find your time and stick to it.

PREPARING FOR AN ESTATE-PLANNING CONFERENCE WITH YOUR ATTORNEY

In preparing for an estate-planning conference with your attorney, you will need the following documents and information for *both* spouses. Place a check (✓) for each document/record you and your spouse have. Add a second check (✓✓) when the information is in hand.

Self	Spouse	
		1. Legal name, permanent address, date and place of birth
		2. Date and place of marriage; if divorced or separated, provide details
		3. Pre/Postnuptial agreements
		4. Names and addresses of children
		5. Employment information
		6. Wills
		7. Names and address of persons to be your executor, guardian, trustee
		8. Income tax returns for the last three years
		9. Gift tax returns
		10. Life insurance policies of both spouses and children
		11. Pensions, profit-sharing, and deferred compensation plans
		12. Business agreements relating to interests in corporations, partnerships, and sole proprietorships
		13. Trust agreements
		14. Buy/sell stock redemption agreements
		15. Real estate, type of ownership, present fair market value mortgages
		16. Other assets, type of ownership, present fair market value
		17. Names and addresses of churches, denominational institutions, and other charities to which you may wish to make a gift

Record date each time information is updated.

_____ _____ _____ _____

_____ _____ _____ _____

KEY ADVISORS

ADVISOR	NAME	ADDRESS	TELEPHONE
Account			
Attorney			
Banker/ Trust Officer			
Business Associates			
Clergyperson			
Doctor			
Funeral Director			
Insurance Agent			
Stockbroker			
Other			
Other			
Other			

Record date each time information is updated.

_____ _____ _____ _____

_____ _____ _____ _____

FAMILY INFORMATION

	Self	*Spouse*
Name		
Address		
Telephone		
Present occupation/Employer		
Address		
Telephone		
Social Security Number		
Date of birth		
Place of birth		
Citizenship		
Date of marriage		
Place of marriage		

Our Children	*Address*	*Date and Place of Birth*
1.		
2.		
3.		
4.		
5.		

My Children		
1.		
2.		
3.		
4.		
5.		

Spouse's Children		
1.		
2.		
3.		
4.		
5.		

Grandchildren's *Parents*	*Grandchildren*	*Date & Place* *of Birth*
M_____	1._____	_____
F_____	2._____	_____
	3._____	_____
	4._____	_____
M_____	1._____	_____
F_____	2._____	_____
	3._____	_____
	4._____	_____
M_____	1._____	_____
F_____	2._____	_____
	3._____	_____
	4._____	_____
M_____	1._____	_____
F_____	2._____	_____
	3._____	_____
	4._____	_____

My Parents	*Spouse's Parents*
Father_____	_____
Address_____	_____
_____	_____
Telephone_____	_____
Date/Place of birth_____	_____
Mother_____	_____
Address_____	_____
_____	_____
Telephone_____	_____
Date/Place of birth_____	_____

Record date each time information is updated.

_____ _____ _____ _____

_____ _____ _____ _____

OBJECTIVES FOR DISTRIBUTING MY ESTATE

	Person	Address/Phone	Relation	Amt/%	Kind
How are assets to be distributed upon death?					
Do you contemplate any lifetime gifts? Give details.					
If you have minor children and you and your spouse both die simultaneously, should assets be held until they reach a certain age? List instructions.					
Are you confident that your spouse is a good manager if he or she survives you? Whom do you suggest your spouse use for help in managing your estate?					
Do your children have any special physical or educational needs? Give details.					
If your spouse survives you, does he or she expect to live in your present home? Give details.					
What gifts do you contemplate to your church or other charitable organizations?	Gifts during lifetime - Gifts upon death - Gifts upon spouse's death -				
Other					

Record date each time information is updated.

_____ _____ _____ _____

_____ _____ _____ _____

OBJECTIVES FOR DISTRIBUTING SPOUSE'S ESTATE

	Person	Address/Phone	Relation	Amt/%	Kind
How are assets to be distributed upon death?					
Do you contemplate any lifetime gifts? Give details.					
If you have minor children and you and your spouse both die simultaneously, should assets be held until they reach a certain age? List instructions.					
Are you confident that your spouse is a good manager if he or she survives you? Whom do you suggest your spouse use for help in managing your estate?					
Do your children have any special physical or educational needs? Give details.					
If your spouse survives you, does he or she expect to live in your present home? Give details.					
What gifts do you contemplate to your church or other charitable organizations?	Gifts during lifetime - Gifts upon death - Gifts upon spouse's death -				
Other					

Record date each time information is updated.

_____ _____ _____ _____

_____ _____ _____ _____

CASH NEEDS NOW, AT RETIREMENT, AND AT DEATH

Sources of Income	Now		At Retirement		At Death	
	Self	Spouse	Self	Spouse	Self	Spouse
Salaries						
Interest						
Dividends						
Rental Properties						
Businesses						
Trusts						
Pensions						
Social Security						
Other						
Total						

Expenses	Now		At Retirement		At Death	
	Self	Spouse	Self	Spouse	Self	Spouse
Standard of Living						
Food						
Mortgages/Rent						
Real Estate Taxes						
Utilities						
Clothing						
Contributions						
Gifts						
Income Taxes						
Loans						
Education						
Insurance						
IRA						
Keogh						
Investments						
Other						
Total						
Excess (Deficit)						

Location of papers_____

Record date each time information is updated.

_____ _____ _____ _____

_____ _____ _____ _____

CURRENT EMPLOYMENT RECORD

Position_____

Employer_____

Address_____Telephone _____

Annual compensation_____

Employment started_____

Immediate supervisor_____

Probable retirement date_____

I participate in these benefit plans through my employer:

☐ Blue Cross

☐ Blue Shield

☐ Major Medical (Company_____)

☐ Pension Plan

☐ Accident Insurance

☐ Disability Plan

☐ Other

☐ Prescription Insurance

☐ Dental Insurance

☐ Credit Union

☐ Profit-Sharing

☐ Stock Purchase

☐ Life Insurance ($_____)

☐ Other

Persons to administer benefit plans:

Name_____ Telephone _____

Address_____

Information booklets on these plans located at_____

_____

Union member ☐ No ☐ Yes   Name/Local #_____

List any union benefits:

Benefits	When Available	Location
_____	_____	_____
_____	_____	_____
_____	_____	_____

List any personal items in office of employment:

Item	Location
_____	_____
_____	_____

How employment ends:

☐ Retirement   ☐ Resignation for other employment   ☐ _____

Record date each time information is updated.

_____ _____ _____ _____

_____ _____ _____ _____

SPOUSE'S CURRENT EMPLOYMENT RECORD

Position_____

Employer_____

Address_____Telephone _____

Annual compensation_____

Employment started_____

Immediate supervisor_____

Probable retirement date_____

I participate in these benefit plans through my employer:

☐ Blue Cross   ☐ Prescription Insurance

☐ Blue Shield   ☐ Dental Insurance

☐ Major Medical (Company_____)   ☐ Credit Union

☐ Pension Plan   ☐ Profit-Sharing

☐ Accident Insurance   ☐ Stock Purchase

☐ Disability Plan   ☐ Life Insurance ($_____)

☐ Other   ☐ Other

Persons to administer benefit plans:

Name_____Telephone _____

Address_____

Information booklets on these plans located at_____

_____

Union member ☐ No ☐ Yes   Name/Local #_____

List any union benefits:

Benefits	When Available	Location
_____	_____	_____
_____	_____	_____
_____	_____	_____

List any personal items in office of employment:

Item	Location
_____	_____
_____	_____
_____	_____

How employment ends:
    ☐ Retirement   ☐ Resignation for other employment   ☐ _____

Record date each time information is updated.

_____ _____ _____ _____

_____ _____ _____ _____

MILITARY SERVICE RECORD

	Self	Spouse
Branch of Service		
Serial number		
Dates and years of service		
Place served, dates, rank		
Place served, dates, rank		
Place served, dates, rank		
Highest rank received		
Date and kind of discharge		
Location of papers		

Military insurance, retirement, and other benefits that are in effect today or will be in the future

	Self	Spouse
Benefit		
Amount		
Date effective		
Location of papers		
Benefit		
Amount		
Date effective		
Location of papers		

For information and assistance, write, telephone, or visit the local or state office of Veteran's Administration:

> Benefit Director
> Veteran's Administration
> 810 Vermont Avenue NE
> Washington, D.C. 20002
> Telephone (202) 393-4120

Record date each time information is updated.

_____   _____   _____   _____

_____   _____   _____   _____

SOCIAL SECURITY EARNINGS RECORD AND PROJECTED BENEFITS

Use information in "Planning with Social Security" to request a statement of earnings and projected benefits every two to three years and record.

Date	Earnings Record		Projected Benefits	
	Self	Spouse	Self	Spouse

Location of record and estimate_____

REAL ESTATE AND STOCKS

Property/ Location	Date Acquired	Cost	Owned By			Possible Change & Costs
		Assessed Value	Self	Spouse	Jointly	
Real Estate						
Stocks						

Record date each time information is updated.

_____ _____ _____ _____

_____ _____ _____ _____

_____ _____ _____ _____

TANGIBLE PERSONAL PROPERTY

Date Acquired	Item/ Location	Purchased from Gifted by	Cost Assessed Value	Owned by		
				Self	Spouse	Jointly

Record date each time information is updated.

_____ _____ _____ _____

_____ _____ _____ _____

MUTUAL FUNDS

Name of fund_____

Date of purchase_____

Number of shares_____

Cost_____

Account number_____

Other specifics:_____

(Leverage Funding, etc.)

Location of papers_____

Record data as account status notices are received.

Date	Income Dividend		Total Received	Capital Gains Distribution	Number of Shares Received	Total Number of Shares Held	Value Per Share	Total Value of Shares
	Qualified / Non-qualified							
								$
								$
								$
								$
								$
								$
								$
								$
								$
								$

SAVINGS BONDS

Date	Series Number	Owners/Beneficiaries	Maturity Date	Location

Record date each time information is updated.

_____ _____ _____ _____

_____ _____ _____ _____

BUSINESS INTEREST CLOSELY HELD

Record information using form for each business interest.

Business_____ Percent owned _____
Type   ☐ Corporation   ☐ Partnership   ☐ Sole proprietorship
Date interest acquired _____ Cost basis of interest _____
Fair market value estimate_____
Give plans if disposing of business interest during lifetime _____
_____
_____

Disposing of business interest at death, I would like to:

	Name	*Address*	*Telephone*

☐ Transfer to family_____

☐ Sell to co-owners_____

☐ Sell to employee_____

Other_____

Does any buy/sell or redemption agreement exist? ☐ Yes   ☐ No
Location of financial statements, tax returns, and any buy/sell or redemption agreements (a copy of each financial statement and tax return for the last five years should be provided for your estate-planning advisor).

Record date each time information is updated.

_____ _____ _____ _____

_____ _____ _____ _____

SPOUSE'S BUSINESS INTEREST CLOSELY HELD

Record information using form for each business interest.

Business_____ Percent owned _____

Type   ☐ Corporation   ☐ Partnership   ☐ Sole proprietorship

Date interest acquired _____ Cost basis of interest _____

Fair market value estimate _____

Give plans if disposing of business interest during lifetime _____

_____

_____

Disposing of business interest at death, I would like to:

	Name	*Address*	*Telephone*
☐ Transfer to family			
☐ Sell to co-owners			
☐ Sell to employee			
Other			

Does any buy/sell or redemption agreement exist? ☐ Yes   ☐ No

Location of financial statements, tax returns, and any buy/sell or redemption agreements (a copy of each financial statement and tax return for the last five years should be provided for your estate-planning advisor).

Record date each time information is updated.

_____   _____   _____   _____

_____   _____   _____   _____

FAMILY LIFE INSURANCE

Life Insurance Provided by Employer

	Self	Spouse
Company		
Policy #		
Type		
Owner		
Beneficiary		
2nd beneficiary		
Face value		
Amount of loan		
Employee's contribution		
Location of policy		

Life Insurance on Self	#1	#2	#3	#4
Company				
Policy #				
Type				
Owner				
Beneficiary				
2nd beneficiary				
Face value				
Cash surrender value/Date				
Amount of loan				
Annual premium				
Location of policy				

Life Insurance on Spouse	#1	#2	#3	#4
Company				
Policy #				
Type				
Owner				
Beneficiary				
2nd beneficiary				
Face value				
Cash surrender value/Date				
Amount of loan				
Annual premium				
Location of policy				

Life Insurance on Children	#1	#2	#3	#4
Company				
Policy #				
Type				
Owner				
Beneficiary				
2nd beneficiary				
Face value				
Cash surrender value/Date				
Amount of loan				
Annual premium				
Location of policy				

Record date each time information is updated.

_____ _____ _____ _____

_____ _____ _____ _____

BANKING INFORMATION

Checking Accounts

Account #_____   Account #_____

Account name_____   Account name_____

Bank_____   Bank_____

Address_____   Address_____

Telephone_____   Telephone_____

Location of book_____   Location of book_____

Account #_____   Account #_____

Account name_____   Account name_____

Bank_____   Bank_____

Address_____   Address_____

Telephone_____   Telephone_____

Location of book_____   Location of book_____

Savings Accounts

Account #_____   Account #_____

Account name_____   Account name_____

Bank_____   Bank_____

Address_____   Address_____

Telephone_____   Telephone_____

Location of book_____   Location of book_____

Account #_____   Account #_____

Account name_____   Account name_____

Bank_____   Bank_____

Address_____   Address_____

Telephone_____   Telephone_____

Location of book_____   Location of book_____

Record date each time information is updated.

_____   _____   _____   _____

_____   _____   _____   _____

A POWER OF ATTORNEY issued on ____ / ____ / _____ until ____ / ____ / _____
authorizes _____ to sign checks, open safe-deposit boxes,
withdraw monies, etc.

Location of document_____

Saving accounts held as security:

Account Number	Date	Bank	Amount	Reason	Location of papers

PERSONAL/BANK LOANS

Type of loan_____

Date_____

Amount_____

Due_____

Payable to_____

Interest rate_____

Security, if any_____

Security held by_____

Location of papers_____

Fully Repaid ☐ Yes ☐ No Date_____

Type of loan_____

Date_____

Amount_____

Due_____

Payable to_____

Interest rate_____

Security, if any_____

Security held by_____

Location of papers_____

Fully Repaid ☐ Yes ☐ No Date_____

Type of loan_____

Date_____

Amount_____

Due_____

Payable to_____

Interest rate_____

Security, if any_____

Security held by_____

Location of papers_____

Fully Repaid ☐ Yes ☐ No Date_____

Type of loan_____

Date_____

Amount_____

Due_____

Payable to_____

Interest rate_____

Security, if any_____

Security held by_____

Location of papers_____

Fully Repaid ☐ Yes ☐ No Date_____

Record date each time information is updated.

_____ _____ _____ _____

_____ _____ _____ _____

SAFE-DEPOSIT BOXES

Box #_____   Box #_____

Bank_____   Bank_____

Address_____   Address_____

Telephone_____   Telephone_____

Contact_____   Contact_____

Box in the name(s) of_____   Box in the name(s) of_____

_____   _____

Person(s) having access_____   Person(s) having access_____

_____   _____

_____   _____

Location(s) of keys_____   Location(s) of keys_____

_____   _____

Contents   ### *Contents*

_____   _____
_____   _____
_____   _____
_____   _____
_____   _____
_____   _____
_____   _____
_____   _____
_____   _____

Record date each time information is updated.

_____   _____   _____   _____

_____   _____   _____   _____

GIFTS MADE DURING LIFETIME

List any gifts (other than charitable gifts) made during your life which exceed $10,000 in value, or $20,000 in value if made jointly with your spouse.

Gift	Date	Value	To	Given by			Gift Tax Return	
				Self	Spouse	Jointly	Federal	State

Gifts that Create a Trust	Date	Location of Trust Document

Gifts Made Under Uniform Gifts to Minors Act

If you and spouse are custodians, give details of property.

Record date each time information is updated.

_____ _____ _____ _____

_____ _____ _____ _____

PLANNING CHARITABLE GIFTS

I express my faith in Christ through the stewardship of accumulating resources.

MYSELF
Some of my dreams about the Christian faith are_____
_____
_____

Some of the ministries I believe in:

1. My local church(es)_____
_____

2._____
_____

3._____
_____

4._____
_____

5._____
_____

I would like to express my faith in Christ in the following ways:

1. Lifetime gifts to:_____
_____

2. Gifts upon death to:_____
_____

3. Gifts upon spouse's death to:_____
_____

4. Gifts that will provide an income for my life (and the life of my spouse or other person) and then be used for:_____
_____
_____

SPOUSE

Some of my dreams about the Christian faith are_____

_____

_____

Some of the ministries I believe in:

1. My local church(es)_____

_____

2._____

_____

3._____

_____

4._____

_____

5._____

_____

I would like to express my faith in Christ in the following ways:

1. Lifetime gifts to:_____

_____

2. Gifts upon death to:_____

_____

3. Gifts upon spouse's death to:_____

_____

4. Gifts that will provide an income for my life (and the life of my spouse or other person) and
   then be used for:_____

_____

_____

Record date each time information is updated.

_____   _____   _____   _____

_____   _____   _____   _____

RECORD OF CHARITABLE GIFTS

Record here any charitable gifts made during your lifetime or planned upon death. There are three categories: (1) Immediate Gifts, (2) Life Income Agreement Gifts, and (3) Gifts Upon Death.

1. IMMEDIATE GIFTS

CASH

Date	Amount	To	Purpose

SECURITIES

Date	# of Shares	Cost Basis	Current Value	To	Purpose

REAL PROPERTY

Date	Description	Location	Cost Basis	Current Value	To	Purpose

PERSONAL PROPERTY

Date	Description	Location	Cost Basis	Current Value	To	Purpose

2. LIFE INCOME AGREEMENT GIFTS

POOLED INCOME FUNDS

Date	Amount	Trustee	Life Beneficiaries	Charitable Beneficiaries & Purpose	Date Income Began

GIFT ANNUITY

Date	Amount	Annual Income	Tax-free Portion	Trustee	Life Beneficiaries	Charitable Beneficiaries & Purpose	Date Income Began

DEFERRED GIFT ANNUITY

Date	Amount	Annual Income	Tax-free Portion	Trustee	Life Beneficiaries	Charitable Beneficiaries & Purpose	Date Income Began

CHARITABLE REMAINDER TRUST (Unitrust and Annuity Trust)

Date	Amount	Income % or $	Trustee	Life Beneficiaries	Charitable Beneficiaries & Purpose	Date Income Began

GIFT OF PERSONAL RESIDENCE WHILE RETAINING LIFE INTEREST

Date	Description	Location	Value	Charitable Beneficiaries & Purpose

3. GIFTS UPON DEATH

BEQUEST IN WILL

Date	Bequest	Estimated Value	Charitable Beneficiaries & Purpose

REVOCABLE TRUST (Made Now, Operable on Death)

Date	Amount	Trustee	Income	Beneficiaries	Charitable Beneficiaries & Purpose

ESTIMATING YOUR FEDERAL TAXABLE ESTATE

The following is only an estimate, but it may help in planning and decision making. If **married,** estimate both estates and what changes may occur in the estate of the second to **die.**

	Self	Spouse
1. Cash in checking and savings accounts	$———	$———
2. Face value of life insurance policies	———	———
3. Fair market value of your homes and other real estate	———	———
4. Fair market value of major personal assets—car, furniture, etc.	———	———
5. Pension plans, death benefits	———	———
6. Fair market value of investments	———	———
7. Other assets	———	———
8. Total—your gross estate	$———	$———
9. Less burial and final costs (perhaps 8 percent of gross estate)	———	———
10. Less unpaid debts, mortgages, taxes	———	———
11. Less charitable gifts	———	———
12. Adjusted gross estate	$———	$———
13. Deduct appropriate unlimited marital deduction if applicable	———	———
14. Net taxable estate	$———	$———
15. Estimated tax owed (see the "Federal Estate and Gift Tax Rates" table)	———	———
16. Deduct available unified credit (see the "Unified Credit Against Federal Estate and Gift Taxes" table)	———	———
17. Estimated tax due	$———	$———

Record date each time information is updated.

—————————— —————————— —————————— ——————————

—————————— —————————— —————————— ——————————

PERSONS TO NOTIFY UPON DEATH

Myself

Name	Relationship	Address	Telephone

Spouse

Name	Relationship	Address	Telephone

Record date each time information is updated.

_____ _____ _____ _____

_____ _____ _____ _____

XIII. Tables

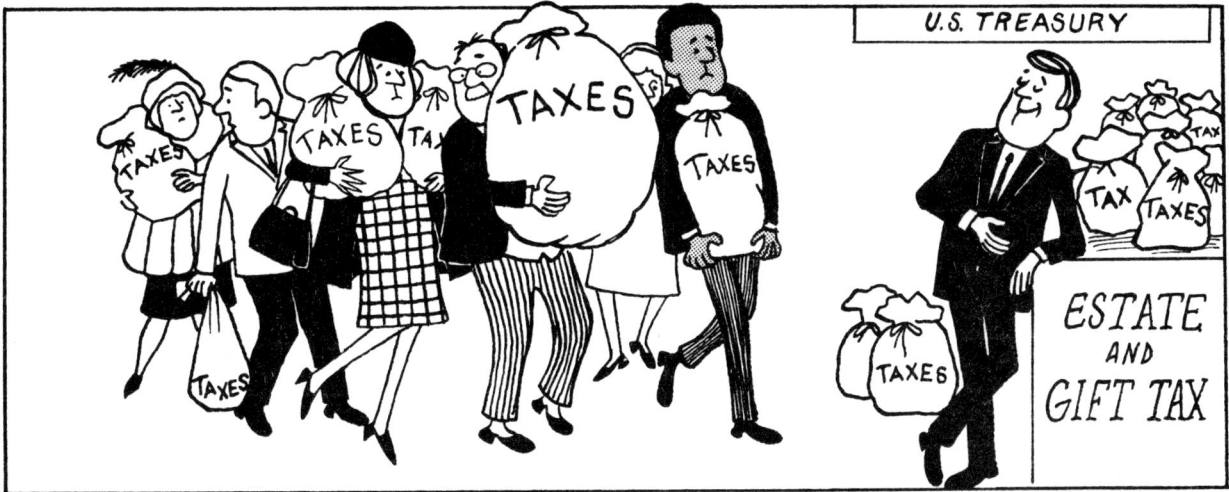

The following tables contain information that may be useful in estate planning. Since federal and state laws change frequently, it is necessary to check the current accuracy of this information with your advisors. A local public library or state law library may contain the information you seek. Be sure to check the publication date of any resource and ask for the recent updated supplements. You may wish to write the approriate federal or state office for information. The state division of revenue will have information about the state's estate or inheritance rate and due date. A county or township register of wills can tell you the executor's commission, other fees, the right of a nonresident to serve as executor, etc.

UNIFIED CREDIT AGAINST FEDERAL ESTATE AND GIFT TAXES

For estates of persons dying in:	the credit is:	or an equivalent exemption of:
1981	$ 47,000	$175,625
1982	62,800	225,000
1983	79,300	275,000
1984	96,300	325,000
1985	121,800	400,000
1986	155,800	500,000
1987	192,800	600,000

FEDERAL ESTATE AND GIFT TAX RATES

This uniform rate table is to be used to calculate both estate and gift taxes.

1982

If the amount is:		Tentative tax[1] is:			
Over	But not over	Tax	+	%	On Excess Over
0	S 10,000	0		18	0
S 10,000	20,000	S 1,800		20	S 10,000
20,000	40,000	3,800		22	20,000
40,000	60,000	8,200		24	40,000
60,000	80,000	13,000		26	60,000
80,000	100,000	18,200		28	80,000
100,000	150,000	23,800		30	100,000
150,000	250,000	38,800		32	150,000
250,000	500,000	70,800		34	250,000
500,000	750,000	155,800		37	500,000
750,000	1,000,000	248,300		39	750,000
1,000,000	1,250,000	345,800		41	1,000,000
1,250,000	1,500,000	448,300		43	1,250,000
1,500,000	2,000,000	555,800		45	1,500,000
2,000,000	2,500,000	780,800		49	2,000,000
2,500,000	3,000,000	1,025,800		53	2,500,000
3,000,000	3,500,000	1,290,800		57	3,000,000
3,500,000	4,000,000	1,575,800		61	3,500,000
4,000,000	....	1,880,800		65	4,000,000

1983

If the amount is:		Tentative tax[1] is:			
Over	But not over	Tax	+	%	On Excess Over
0	S 10,000	0		18	0
S 10,000	20,000	S 1,800		20	S 10,000
20,000	40,000	3,800		22	20,000
40,000	60,000	8,200		24	40,000
60,000	80,000	13,000		26	60,000
80,000	100,000	18,200		28	80,000
100,000	150,000	23,800		30	100,000
150,000	250,000	38,800		32	150,000
250,000	500,000	70,800		34	250,000
500,000	750,000	155,800		37	500,000
750,000	1,000,000	248,300		39	750,000
1,000,000	1,250,000	345,800		41	1,000,000
1,250,000	1,500,000	448,300		43	1,250,000
1,500,000	2,000,000	555,800		45	1,500,000
2,000,000	2,500,000	780,800		49	2,000,000
2,500,000	3,000,000	1,025,800		53	2,500,000
3,000,000	3,500,000	1,290,800		57	3,000,000
3,500,000	....	1,575,800		60	3,500,000

[1]The cumulated transfers to which the tentative tax applies are the sum of (a) the amount of the taxable estate and (b) the amount of the taxable gifts made by the decedent after 1976 other than gifts includible in the gross estate.

1984

| If the amount is: | | Tentative tax[1] is: | | |
Over	But not over	Tax +	%	On Excess Over
0	$ 10,000	0	18	0
$ 10,000	20,000	$ 1,800	20	$ 10,000
20,000	40,000	3,800	22	20,000
40,000	60,000	8,200	24	40,000
60,000	80,000	13,000	26	60,000
80,000	100,000	18,200	28	80,000
100,000	150,000	23,800	30	100,000
150,000	250,000	38,800	32	150,000
250,000	500,000	70,800	34	250,000
500,000	750,000	155,800	37	500,000
750,000	1,000,000	248,300	39	750,000
1,000,000	1,250,000	345,800	41	1,000,000
1,250,000	1,500,000	448,300	43	1,250,000
1,500,000	2,000,000	555,800	45	1,500,000
2,000,000	2,500,000	780,800	49	2,000,000
2,500,000	3,000,000	1,025,800	53	2,500,000
3,000,000	....	1,290,800	55	3,000,000

1985 and Thereafter

| If the amount is: | | Tentative tax[1] is: | | |
Over	But not over	Tax +	%	On Excess Over
0	$ 10,000	0	18	0
$ 10,000	20,000	$ 1,800	20	$ 10,000
20,000	40,000	3,800	22	20,000
40,000	60,000	8,200	24	40,000
60,000	80,000	13,000	26	60,000
80,000	100,000	18,200	28	80,000
100,000	150,000	23,800	30	100,000
150,000	250,000	38,800	32	150,000
250,000	500,000	70,800	34	250,000
500,000	750,000	155,800	37	500,000
750,000	1,000,000	248,300	39	750,000
1,000,000	1,250,000	345,800	41	1,000,000
1,250,000	1,500,000	448,300	43	1,250,000
1,500,000	2,000,000	555,800	45	1,500,000
2,000,000	2,500,000	780,800	49	2,000,000
2,500,000	....	1,025,800	50	2,500,000

[1]The cumulated transfers to which the tentative tax applies are the sum of (a) the amount of the taxable estate and (b) the amount of the taxable gifts made by the decedent after 1976 other than gifts includible in the gross estate.

Section 2001 of the Internal Revenue Code 1954 as subsequently amended.

XIV. Estate-planning Terms

Administrator/Administratrix........ A person appointed by a court to administer and settle the estate of a person dying without a will or the estate of a person whose will appoints an executor/executrix who declines or is unable to serve.

Alternate Executor/Executrix...... A person nominated in a will to serve as executor/executrix if nominated executor/executrix is unable or declines to serve.

Annual Exclusion........................ The first $10,000 given in any year by one person to any number of others is excluded from the gift tax. Husband and wife may exclude $20,000 given jointly to the same persons.

Appointed Property..................... Property held under a power of appointment.

Appointee................................... A person to whom property has been appointed through a power of appointment.

Assets... Property—real and personal, tangible and intangible.

Asset Replenishing..................... The replenishment of a gifted asset using after-tax income from a charitable gift annuity gifted to heirs to purchase whole life insurance placed in an irrevocable insurance trust.

Bargain Sale............................... Sale of property to a charity for less than the fair market value. The difference between the selling price and fair market value is considered a charitable contribution.

Bequest...................................... A gift of personal property by will.

Bond.. A written obligation to pay money or to perform duties usually guaranteed by the signature of another person or a corporation. In estate planning, bond usually refers to the obligation of an administrator, guardian, executor, or trustee in performing duties.

Carryover...................................... The right to carry over any excess charitable contribution deduction for five succeeding years.

Charitable Deduction.................... An income or estate tax deduction based on the value of property irrevocably given to an approved charity.

Charitable Remainder Trust........ A trust agreement under which income is paid to one or more persons for life after which the gift belongs to the charity.

Clifford Trust.............................. Short-term trust that pays income to another person for ten or more years after which it reverts to the person creating the trust.

Codicil.. An addition to a will that modifies or revokes an existing provision but does not change the entire will.

Common Stock.............................. Stock that represents a share of ownership in a corporation.

Community Property.................... Law in Arizona, California, Idaho, Louisiana, New Mexico, Nevada, Texas, and Washington that provides for property acquired by either spouse during marriage to be held in common with a half interest each.

Cosanguinity................................ Degrees of blood relationships of persons.

Corpus... The main body or principal of a trust. The principal sum or capital, as distingushed from interest or income.

Cost Basis..................................... The purchase cost of securities, real estate, or personal property.

Crummey Powers.......................... The equivocal right to make withdrawals from an irrevocable insurance trust that are necessary to obtain gift tax exclusion for transfer of policy and premiums.

Curtesy.. The right arising from marriage of a husband in his wife's property.

Direct Charitable Deduction........ A direct charitable contribution deduction available for taxpayers who do not itemize deductions. It is provided by the Economic Recovery Tax Act of 1981 and is available the tax years 1982 through 1986.

Disclaimer.................................. Refusal of an estate or of an interest in property.

Donee... A person to whom a gift is made.

Donor... A person who makes a gift.

Dower.. The right arising from marriage of a wife in her husband's property.

Entirety..................................... That which the law considers whole and cannot be divided.

Estate.. All property—real and personal—owned by a person.

Estate Planning......................... A plan for managing, preserving, and transferring property during life and upon death.

Estate Tax................................. A tax on the right to transfer property to others at death.

Executor/Executrix..................... A person nominated in a will to carry out the directions of the will.

Federal Adjusted Gross Estate.... The federal gross estate less funeral and administration expenses, claims against the estate, and debts.

Fee Simple................................. Outright ownership of land.

Fiduciary................................... An administrator, guardian, executor, or trustee whose duty is to act for the benefit of another.

Future Interest.......................... Interest in real or personal property in which possession or enjoyment begins at some future time.

Gift Annuity.............................. An agreement with a charity whereby income from a gift is paid to one or two persons for life at a fixed annual amount. The rates paid can be based on the age of the donor and tables of the Conference on Gift Annuities.

Gift Tax.................................... A tax imposed by the federal government and some states on the transfer of property during lifetime. The federal tax is imposed on the donor. In some states the tax is imposed on the donee.

Gifts to Minors Act..................... An act adopted in most states providing for transferring property (usually stocks and bonds) to minors; the legal custodian has the right to act without a guardianship.

Guardian................................... A person appointed by a court to take custody of the person, estate, or both, of an infant or incompetent person.

Holographic Will............................A handwritten will with the signature of the person writing it.

Incidents of Ownership...............Incidents of ownership in life insurance are any power over the policy and its benefits. This includes power to change beneficiary, to borrow, or to assign, surrender, cancel, or revoke an assignment.

Inheritance...................................Property received from one who dies.

Inheritance Tax...........................A tax on the right to receive property from a decedent.

Instrument...................................A written legal document.

Inter Vivos Trust.........................A trust created during lifetime in which property is placed with a trustee for the benefit of another, oneself, or object.

Intestate......................................Dying without a will.

Irrevocable..................................An agreement which cannot be changed or revoked.

Joint Tenants with
Right of Survivorship..................Persons (two or more) who hold title jointly with equal shares during life and with the survivor receiving the entire property.

Life Estate..................................Property held only for life of one or more persons; it then goes to someone else.

Life Interest................................A claim in real or personal property limited by a term of life.

Living Will..................................A request in writing to not prolong life by artificial means when death is certain.

Marital Deduction........................A deduction from the federal gross estate for gifts to a spouse during lifetime or for property passing to the surviving spouse upon death. The 1981 Tax Act made this deduction unlimited.

Personal Property.........................Everything owned other than real estate.

Per Stirpes..................................The share a parent would have taken goes to his or her descendants.

Pooled Income Fund.....................A trust funded by a number of donors who receive a pro rata share of the earnings each year for life and the life of a survivor when desired. At death, the value of the donor's share will be transferred to a charity chosen by the donor.

Pour-over Will.............................A will which leaves all or part of an estate to a trustee under an inter vivos trust.

Power of Appointment.................A power given to a person (donee of the power) to decide who receives the property of the one giving the power. The power of appointment may be general or specific.

Probate...The court process of proving a will valid or invalid and the administration of the estate of a decedent.

Qualified Terminable Interest......Property that passes from the decedent and in which the surviving spouse has a qualifying income interest for life. The election to have such an interest qualify for the marital deduction must be made by the executor on the federal estate tax form. Once the election is made it is irrevocable.

Real Property...............................Real estate—property in land and buildings.

Right of Election
Against the Will...........................The surviving spouse may elect to take the statutory share in assets of a decedent's estate instead of the share under the will.

Settlor..A person who creates a trust. Also called *creator, donor, trustor*.

Tenancy by the Entirety..............A form of ownership created by husband and wife to the whole property with right of survivorship.

Terminable Interest......................An interest in property that terminates upon the holder's death or at another specified time.

Totten Trust................................A trust in the form of a bank account that passes to the named beneficiary upon death of the grantor.

Unified Credit..............................A credit against the unified Federal Estate Gift tax, provided by the Tax Reform Act of 1976 and increased by the Economic Recovery Tax Act of 1981.

Will...A legal document specifying the disposition of property after death. It is revocable during life.